PRAISE FOR *BATTLE CRY*

"You deserve to be free, yet as men, most of us weren't taught how to process the emotional pain and trauma we experience. In *Battle Cry*, Jason's leadership and wisdom shine through as he gives us the mental weapons and emotional stability needed to wage and win the war within all of us. If you want to feel free, this book will teach you how fight the right way and keep your freedom!"

—LEWIS HOWES, ENTREPRENEUR AND *NEW YORK TIMES* BESTSELLING AUTHOR OF *THE SCHOOL OF GREATNESS*

"Jason Wilson is a man who grew up with experiences similar to many men in society. But unlike most men, he has found the quaesitum to the problem of men suppressing their emotions to seem more 'manly.' He is a person that I come to and absorb knowledge about life. Since knowing and following him I have become more conscious of my mind and emotions. This book will edify whoever reads it, empowering them to master their emotions and live free of the judgements of society."

—TREY FLOWERS, TWO-TIME NFL SUPER BOWL CHAMPION

"Every man is in a war. Many of us fight, but many of us don't know how to win. Enter Jason Wilson—Jason is our guide. His words bring hope and healing. This book does the same. *Battle Cry* is more than just a title; it's a call for all of mankind. A call to be the men God intended. In *Battle Cry*, Jason teaches us how to win the war within our hearts, minds, and souls. As a young man trying to figure it all out, I couldn't be happier that this book is here. Thank you, Jason, for teaching me how to be a good man."

—SAM ACHO, AUTHOR, SPEAKER, AND NINE-YEAR NFL LINEBACKER

"We are in a global mental health crisis and Jason Wilson is on the frontlines making a difference by delivering real solutions. Jason is the leading expert in helping men break through with their emotions and his new book will inspire men to yell a battle cry and win the war within!"

—MEL ROBBINS, *NEW YORK TIMES* BESTSELLING AUTHOR OF *THE 5 SECOND RULE*

"Once again Jason Wilson has inspired us to lean into our vulnerabilities and release the trauma that causes wars to wage within us daily. His leadership, transparency, and examples in *Battle Cry* are touchstones for the modern man navigating the reality of parenting, partnership, and purpose!"

—SHAKA SENGHOR, *NEW YORK TIMES* BESTSELLING AUTHOR OF *WRITING MY WRONGS*

BATTLE CRY

WAGING AND WINNING
THE WAR WITHIN

JASON WILSON

NELSON
BOOKS
An Imprint of Thomas Nelson

Published in Nashville, Tennessee, by Nelson Books, an imprint of Thomas Nelson. Nelson Books and Thomas Nelson are registered trademarks of HarperCollins Christian Publishing, Inc.

Thomas Nelson titles may be purchased in bulk for educational, business, fundraising, or sales promotional use. For information, please email SpecialMarkets@ThomasNelson.com.

Unless otherwise noted, Scripture quotations are taken from the New American Standard Bible®, Copyright © 1960, 1971, 1977, 1995 (NASB) by The Lockman Foundation. Used by permission. All rights reserved. www.lockman.org.

Scripture quotations marked CEV are from the Contemporary English Version. Copyright © 1991, 1992, 1995 by American Bible Society. Used by permission.

Scripture quotations marked ESV are from the ESV® Bible (The Holy Bible, English Standard Version®). Copyright © 2001 by Crossway, a publishing ministry of Good News Publishers. All rights reserved.

Scripture quotations marked KJV are from the King James Version of the Bible. Public Domain.

Scripture quotations marked NIV are from the Holy Bible, New International Version®, NIV®. Copyright © 1973, 1978, 1984, 2011 by Biblica, Inc.® Used by permission of Zondervan. All rights reserved worldwide. www.zondervan.com. The "NIV" and "New International Version" are trademarks registered in the United States Patent and Trademark Office by Biblica, Inc.®

Scripture quotations marked NKJV are from the New King James Version®. Copyright © 1982 by Thomas Nelson. Used by permission. All rights reserved.

Scripture quotations marked NLT are from the Holy Bible, New Living Translation. Copyright © 1996, 2004, 2015 by Tyndale House Foundation. Used by permission of Tyndale House Publishers, Carol Stream, Illinois 60188. All rights reserved.

Scripture quotations marked TLB are from The Living Bible. Copyright © 1971. Used by permission of Tyndale House Publishers, a division of Tyndale House Ministries, Carol Stream, Illinois 60188. All rights reserved.

Any internet addresses, phone numbers, or company or product information printed in this book are offered as a resource and are not intended in any way to be or to imply an endorsement by Thomas Nelson, nor does Thomas Nelson vouch for the existence, content, or services of these sites, phone numbers, companies, or products beyond the life of this book.

Names and identifying characteristics of some individuals have been changed to preserve their privacy.

Emotional Stability Training is a registered trademark and is used with permission.

The information in this book has been carefully researched by the author and is intended to be a source of information only. It is based on the research and observations of the author, who is not a medical doctor. While the methods contained herein can and do work, readers are urged to consult with their physicians or other professional advisors to address specific medical or other issues. The author and the publisher assume no responsibility for any injuries suffered or damages or losses incurred during or as a result of the use or application of the information contained herein.

Library of Congress Cataloging-in-Publication Data

Names: Wilson, Jason, author.
Title: Battle cry : waging and winning the war within / Jason Wilson.
Description: Nashville, Tennessee : Thomas Nelson, [2021] | Includes bibliographical references. | Summary: "Defying a culture that proclaims "real men don't cry," Jason Wilson calls readers to unlearn society's definition of masculinity and discover the freedom and healing of engaging with and mastering their emotions"-- Provided by publisher.
Identifiers: LCCN 2021007477 (print) | LCCN 2021007478 (ebook) | ISBN 9781400226993 (trade paperback) | ISBN 9781400228171 (epub)
Subjects: LCSH: Christian men--Religious life. | Emotions. | Masculinity. | Men--Identity. | BISAC: SELF-HELP / Emotions | SELF-HELP / Communication & Social Skills
Classification: LCC BV4528.2. W529 2021 (print) | LCC BV4528.2 (ebook) | DDC 248.8/42--dc23
LC record available at https://lccn.loc.gov/2021007477
LC ebook record available at https://lccn.loc.gov/2021007478

Printed in the United States of America
21 22 23 24 25 LSC 10 9 8 7 6 5 4 3 2 1

To every man who is tired of not living—don't give up.

CONTENTS

Introduction   ix

ONE Escaping Emotional Incarceration   1

TWO Misconstrued Masculinity   17

THREE Putting Peace in Perspective   33

FOUR Courageous Transparency   49

FIVE Abort Your Shadow Mission   65

SIX Purging Passivity   77

SEVEN Combat Communication   93

EIGHT Sexual Self-Control   111

NINE Accepting Affirmation   129

TEN Rest Now or Rest in Peace   145

ELEVEN Let Go and Live   163

A Final Word   179

Resources   181

Acknowledgments   183

Notes   187

About the Author   192

INTRODUCTION

It's deeply saddening to see so many good men,
even the strong, on the verge of giving up—
no one wants to be the problem all the time.
—*Zaddiyq AriYah*

I t's too late for me to change."

"I want to cry, but I can't."

"I'll look weak if I express how I really feel."

"I'm tired of always being the problem."

"Life is no longer worth living."

I hear heart-rending statements like these every day from men who are suffering in silence, condemning themselves as if they were never allowed to make a mistake. Although they long to express their emotions, the fear of being wrong again or impassively dismissed is enough to tame their desire to be hu*man*. Then there's the other extreme of men who repress their childhood trauma instead of releasing it. Subsequently, they perceive every opposing opinion or minor altercation as disrespect and quickly meet it with an intemperate reaction.

Instead of swatting away the mosquito, these men wait for it to land on a glass table, then kill it with a sledgehammer. They are willing to risk it all to be heard . . . and to be right.

I know both men very well because I use to morph between the two.

For decades, I was a slave to my erratic emotions. Instead of calmly articulating my feelings regarding an offense, I would yell in order to hide that I had been hurt. In the early years of our marriage, my wife, Nicole, and I often got into heated arguments. One afternoon, my emotional instability triggered a strong reaction in me. Our daughter, Alexis, eleven at the time, was upstairs watching television while Nicole and I were in the basement. As our arguing intensified, I walked away to escape Nicole's quick-witted responses, but to no avail—she followed me into the laundry room.

I yelled, "Why don't you just let me be the man and follow my lead!"

With hands on her hips, Nicole sharply responded, "Why don't you lead like one?"

Because I love Nicole deeply, her words hit me as if she had taken a hammer to my chest and shattered my heart. But my ego would not allow me to express the emotional pain I felt, so I stomped up the stairs—and punched a hole in the wall. Nicole uttered sarcastically, "Wow, that's great!"

Enraged at her response, I shouted, "I'll punch holes in all these [expletive] walls!" Within seconds, I punched five holes in the stairwell walls. When I reached the top of the stairs, the sight of fear in my beloved daughter's eyes sobered my soul and made it clear: I'd lost control. After taking time to decompress, Nicole and I reconciled, but because I hadn't dealt with the root cause of our conflict, the peace in our home was brief.

As I look back on all this now, I realize the problem was that I was *emotionally incarcerated*. I shared in my book *Cry Like a Man* that my emotional incarceration meant I was isolated and disconnected from emotions that threatened to consume me. And, sadly, I had been this way since my youth. Our culture admonishes boys for being emotional and promotes the idea that a "real man" is strong at all times. As a result, boys become men who cannot be vulnerable or transparent with their true feelings. Emotions then become like Ping-Pong balls under water. You can only hold them down for so long before one pops up unexpectedly—and often uncontrollably.

Due to the influence of popular culture, men believe they are not allowed to be afraid or feel fear. So instead of contemplating why we are scared, we suppress that emotion because of a deeper fear of being perceived as pusillanimous—timid and spineless. Yet every man at some point in his life will be afraid, especially when he has children. As one of my friends once stated, "Our children are like watching our hearts walk around outside of our bodies." Every mature man admits this is true, but until we are courageously transparent with our feelings, our sons will follow in our footsteps

> **Emotions [are] like Ping-Pong balls under water. You can only hold them down for so long before one pops up unexpectedly—and often uncontrollably.**

and try to be what they perceive us to be—willing to risk their lives and lineage for the sake of appearing brave.

I was deeply moved by Mufasa's transparency in Disney's classic movie *The Lion King* after he watched his only beloved son, Simba, recklessly risk his life trying to prove he was courageous. Simba had assumed that kings were never scared because he never saw his father show fear. But Mufasa knew that if he did not share the truth in the moment, Simba would die young and bring an end to their kingdom.

"Son, I'm only brave when I have to be," Mufasa said.

"But you're not scared of anything!" Simba responded.

"I was today."

"You were?" Simba was clearly surprised by his father's admission.

"I thought I might lose you."[1]

This priceless moment between father and son not only transformed Simba's mindset but also laid a solid foundation for his future.

I know numerous men who still to this day believe their sons should never see them cry or be afraid of anything. This dangerous ideology has produced not only generations of men imprisoned by their emotions, but also early graves. With most men unable to express their emotions in healthy ways, the result we're seeing now is depression, divorce, high-risk behaviors, broken families, and violence. Futures erased. Wounded hearts. Despair.

There is freedom when you allow yourself to feel fear or any emotion that's not considered traditionally masculine. The problem is, we become imprisoned when we succumb to thoughts that keep us from resolutely walking in our purpose.

As a man thinks about himself, so he will be (Prov. 23:7), and it isn't until we actively engage our emotions that we will be able to release negative thoughts before they become toxic actions.

In the United States men die by suicide 3.5 times more often than women,[2] and men commit 75.6 percent of violent crimes.[3] Unfortunately, many people mistakenly believe that men were created to be aggressive and violent, but the truth is that most of us were programmed to process and release our emotional pain in destructive ways. Imagine how many good men would still be living today if they had taken a moment to feel and acknowledge their emotions, instead of dismissing them until they lost control.

The High Cost of Emotional Suppression

It's 5:00 a.m. on Friday, April 10, 2020, and I'm sitting in my office alone. The entire planet is in the midst of the coronavirus pandemic. At the time of this book's writing, there have been more than 12.4 million cases and more than 257,000 deaths related to COVID-19 in the United States. We don't know when the pandemic will end. The world is reeling, and my beloved Detroit is now ranked third in the country for coronavirus deaths.[4] No one in my home has contracted this deadly virus, but our family has lost several loved ones to COVID-19. The sadness, fear, and trauma are palpable.

From sporting events to Hollywood, entertainment has been disrupted. There seems to be no escape, no distraction for our souls and minds. As a result, I receive numerous direct messages daily from emotionally distressed men. Distressed—not by the fear of dying from COVID-19, but by having to be quarantined with their own fears for an indefinite period of time. And, unfortunately, lawyers across the country have reported receiving an unprecedented number of divorce requests since families were ordered to remain inside their homes during the pandemic.

When we hide or deny our negative emotions, they become toxic and fester like infectious wounds. We can only pretend for so long before something erupts, causing regret, shame, and relational turmoil. If we never address the root cause of our pain, our internal wounds will breed like cancer cells. And then, when we're finally forced to face them, we'll start to self-destruct.

Warrior, your relationships are at stake. Your health is at stake. Your future is at stake. You must act now and fight for *your* life with all vigilance. For far too long, I allowed the emergencies of others to take precedence over my own needs. My entire life revolved around helping other people and neglecting myself. I unknowingly based my existence on what I did for others instead of who I was. This birthed resentment in my heart and sapped my desire to live. Drinking beer became psychotherapy, and anger was the only emotion I could express. My unreleased toxic thoughts turned into destructive actions that I regret to this day.

When a man cannot introspectively confront his negative thoughts and emotions, he will always be conquered by them, communicating without composure and hurting those he loves. It wasn't my family or my friends who were responsible for my lack of self-love; it was years of living with unresolved trauma that triggered my unhealthy mental state.

Winning the Introspective War—
Is It Worth the Fight?

It has been said that no matter where you go, there you will be. In other words, we cannot escape ourselves. Therefore it's imperative that we learn how to wage and win the *introspective* war. We need to examine our own mental and emotional states so we can release emotional pain and trauma before we inflict them on others.

Warrior, if you are hurting and hiding, tired of not being able to say you're tired, weak but without the confidence to be strong, strong but with nowhere to go when you're weak, I want you to know: there is a life to live beyond the limitations of what you've been programmed to believe it means to be a man.

I don't claim to have all the answers, but I am a living testimony that you can win this battle. Like me, you must be willing to fight to unlearn what you've been deceived to believe. Since this war is not just mental but also spiritual, you will notice that I refer to Jesus by His Hebrew name, *Yahushua*, and God the Father as *Yah* (short form of *YHWH/Yahuah*), and I'll reference scriptures throughout. Without Yah and His Word, I would have lost my mind a long time ago and forfeited the fulfilling life I am living today.

Please know, my goal is not to proselytize but to give you

> **There is a life to live beyond the limitations of what you've been programmed to believe it means to be a man.**

the weapons of warfare that have worked for me and many other men.

The introspective war is one you will have to fight daily for the rest of your life, so it will take more than faith to win the war within. You will also need to be a man of action—proactively taking captive every negative emotion before it enslaves you (2 Cor. 10:5). In the chapters ahead, I will show you how to do this through stories from my own life and the lives of boys and men I have trained through this process. We'll also dismantle the myths that surround masculinity and keep men imprisoned.

But first, you have to believe that freedom from emotional incarceration is attainable. My intention is not only to empower you with the skills needed to break free but also prove that it is possible for a man to live from the good in his heart and not his fears—regardless of how hopeless life appears right now.

Second, you must understand that this war is not won overnight; it is a journey. In fact, there is no "arriving" at perfection. There is only continued healing and growth. The process of taking hold of your freedom requires examining your unresolved trauma and reflecting on how it negatively affects the way you view yourself, your relationships, and your everyday life.

You will need to release any toxic emotions that come up during your self-examination. This will require gut-level honesty with yourself and others. But I promise that the future you can step into as a result is better than you can imagine.

Are you ready to fight and win the war that will change your life? If so, gather yourself mentally, physically, and emotionally as I take you down the narrow path of training that will empower you to break through what you've been through!

ONE

ESCAPING EMOTIONAL INCARCERATION

My emotions only become my enemy, when
I suppress them within my inner me.
—*Shärath Wilson*

In the United States, the dimensions of a typical prison cell are approximately six by eight feet, encased in steel or brick walls. One solid or barred door locks the cell from the exterior. Those condemned to life inside soon lose touch with the free world outside.

Sadly, there's another prison cell that holds more men captive than all the industrialized prisons in the world. This cellblock is customized for each inmate, with undetectable walls and a solid "mental door" that locks from the inside—keeping the hearts of men isolated from society at large.

What's also extraordinary about this prison cell is that it can only be inhabited by an inmate who voluntarily turns himself in. No warrant, no judge, no jury—just a good man who is tired of fighting to feel. He has suppressed his emotions for so long that he no longer feels them when he does something wrong. In order to keep from hurting others, he subconsciously imprisons himself to a daily life sentence of emotional incarceration. Yes, a daily life sentence because each day when this inmate wakes up, he has an opportunity to walk as a free man, but he's so disempowered he can't find his way out.

Unfortunately, due to the lack of safe spaces for men to express our emotions, we choose to stay incarcerated because it's better than being exposed and humiliated for being imperfect human beings. I say "we" because I, too, was emotionally incarcerated. I started serving my sentence at the age of twelve. Like many boys before they are influenced by this flawed world, I was kindhearted and creative, and I loved helping people. But in the community I grew up in, the hypermasculine black male was the gold standard, and if you failed to meet that criteria, or at least have that appearance, you'd have to fight every day to keep a pretty girlfriend. Not because you weren't attractive enough to have a girl but because you didn't look tough enough to be with her in public.

So, I had to make a decision—either fit in or be an outcast. I chose option one. I went from being on the honor roll to being a regular summer school student. My attitude plummeted, and by the time I reached my teenage years, I had mastered playing the role of a "thug."

I stopped hanging with my friends who were respectful and honored their parents, and I sought camaraderie with gang members on my block. The things that bothered me before no longer did—I became desensitized to bullying, crime, and misogynistic behavior. Evil had become good and good evil. I started carrying illegal weapons and sometimes would sneak out my stepfather's gun to impress my new friends. As the rapper E-40's song advised, I practiced "lookin' hard" in the mirror every day, and as a result, the joyful smile that had once highlighted my face vanished. Although the thug life always felt like a suit too small for a young man with a big heart, I assumed I had no other choice for survival.

Regrettably, I didn't realize what a T.H.U.G. truly was—a Traumatized Human Unable to Grieve—until I began to break free from emotional incarceration. Since crying was universally considered a violation of manhood, those who experienced trauma could never release it. The only tears I saw on a man's face were tattooed—a symbol of death and grief. Until I broke free, I continued to suppress who I really was because living from the heart Yah gave me would have been considered soft by my peers.

Fast-forward to 1997 and that same boy was in a twenty-seven-year-old body. However, this would be the year I would confess with my mouth and believe in my heart that Yahushua is Lord—surrendering my life to the Most High. This conversion set me free from the bondage of sin, but I was still an emotionally incarcerated inmate. Although I made numerous attempts to leave this prison, the fear of being vulnerable was greater than my desire for freedom. Just as a dog returns to his vomit, I returned to my cell day after day. It was not healthy or safe.

Emotional incarceration is a self-imposed mental imprisonment—when a man confines his non-masculine emotions and isolates his heart from the world. It appears to be a "safe space"; however, like the majority of real prisons in the world, this institution does not rehabilitate you. Instead, emotional incarceration breeds what got you sentenced in the first place—passive aggression, unresolved anger, and abandonment, to name a few. Sadly, I chose to get married while locked up in this prison of anger and pain. I was a good man, blessed with a beautiful family. My loving wife, Nicole, and my beautiful daughter, Alexis, would get to visit the real me on my birthday, Father's Day, or any event that made me feel safe enough to come out of my self-imposed cell and express positive emotions such as love, joy, happiness, and gratitude. Nicole and I often had our "conjugal visits," and in 2007, the Most High blessed us with a son, Jason Jr.

My son was truly an answer to prayer because he influenced me to leave my emotional cell more often. But as always, just before sunset, I would embrace Nicole, Alexis, and Jason, and then shrink back into the cell I'd built. Before I would fall asleep, I would ponder how good it felt to be free from depression, hopelessness, confusion, and unresolved anger. And I would wonder, *Why can't I do this all day, every day?* This unhealthy cycle eventually took a toll on my relationship with Nicole, and after seventeen years of marriage, we considered separation.

Some people change when they see the light, while others convert when they feel the heat. I was the latter. I tried my best to "be a man" and hide my feelings again, but the thought of losing my family without a fight was unfathomable. So I decided to walk out of emotional incarceration and step into a boxing ring—or, more accurately, an MMA (mixed martial arts) cage—for the fight of my life. Staying free would require me to grapple with the toxic thought patterns and emotions that kept my brain in a fight-or-flight response.

The fight-or-flight response is the brain's reaction to acute stress, preparing the body to defend itself against danger. When our brains are stuck in this physiological response, emotional intimacy and vulnerability can feel like a threat, resulting in relational conflict and coercing us to live from our fears instead of our hearts.

Hurt people not only hurt people, but they subconsciously keep hurting people. And themselves.

Hurt people not only hurt people, but they subconsciously keep hurting people. And themselves. The conflict inside my mind seemed like a war being waged for my soul, and my psychotherapist, Dr. Tim Broe, confirmed it was.

But why was I still losing this war after I had surrendered my life to the Most High?

Unreleased Trauma

Growing up, I never felt comfortable expressing any emotion that wasn't "masculine." My father and male family members programmed me to "suck it up." It's likely that their fathers and brothers had challenged them to do the same. But hearing this message is like inhaling the fumes from a car's exhaust pipe— you only have so much time before the poisonous gas creates toxicity in your body and you die.

When I was nine years old, I loved being outside with my puppy named Coby. One day Coby got away from me and playfully ran down my block past a group of teenagers. One of the boys attempted to stomp on Coby's leash to stop him from running, but his foot landed on Coby instead, crushing his rib cage. They all laughed as I carried my puppy's limp body home. My mom and I rushed Coby to the vet, but the only option was to put him to sleep. Although my eyes tear up as I type this, I did not cry that day. Instead, the hurt I was taught to suppress became deep-rooted hatred, and I plotted to severely hurt or kill the teenage boy who had stomped the life out of my puppy.

If I had been taught that crying is normal and healthy for men, I could have cried to release the emotional pain of Coby's death, and I probably would have had the capacity to forgive—but I didn't. So, I praise Yah that the boy's family moved off our block a couple of years later.

Hurtful, disappointing, and traumatizing events happen. They are part of life in this imperfect world. But if we have no outlet for our emotional responses, they begin to stack up on top of one another until we feel buried, overwhelmed, bitter, and resentful.

By the time I became a man, I had mastered repressing my humanity and living only from masculine attributes such as strength, courage, and aggression. I had become emotionally imbalanced—unable to express how I really felt, and constipated with cares but refusing an emotional enema.

The hardest thing for a man to do is deal with himself, to confront his own emotional pain and trauma so he can stop inflicting it on others. In many vain attempts to find peace, he's more likely to keep evading the real problem—himself—and perpetually blame others for what he sees in the mirror. In a spiritual context, man is the head of woman (1 Cor. 11:3). However, if the head of the house stays negatively affected by past emotional pain and trauma, those underneath his roof will be traumatized as well.

The human traits of caring, compassion, and empathy are beneficial, especially in relationships, and crying provides a healthy release for trauma. Biochemist Dr. William H. Frey discovered that emotionally induced tears contain not only water but stress hormones that are released from our bodies through crying. Ironically, his research also revealed that people with stress-related illnesses cry less than those who are considered healthy.[1]

The quality of your life is determined by the quality of your emotions. My emotions were destroying my life and taking my family down with me. When it looked like my marriage was going to end, I knew something had to change in me. I couldn't bear the thought of losing Nicole and the family Yah had blessed me with.

Although I alone had to take the first step to emotional freedom, the process of attaining the healing I deeply desired for myself and my family could not be achieved unaided. It is written, "Though one may be overpowered by another, two can withstand him. And a threefold cord is not quickly broken" (Eccl. 4:12 NKJV). When I pursued the professional help of Dr. Tim Broe and camaraderie that welcomed vulnerability, I finally learned how to cry like a man, releasing years of trauma and emotional pain that had been suppressed in my heart and mind.

I was finally free to feel!

The feelings that masqueraded as anger were now liberated to be expressed without fear of looking like I was mentally fragile or milksop. Now that I can verbally process my emotions, Nicole and I no longer guard our hearts from each other. Instead of holding grudges, we embrace our desire to trust each other's intent. The peace in our home is tangible. The release of toxic emotions from my childhood empowers me to parent with patience, and my transparency opened the door for my children to be vulnerable with me as well. All men desire and deserve this kind of peace, and we can attain it if we are willing to fight for it. Since the beginning of man's history, a lack of emotional stability—the ability to confront, conquer, and communicate our emotions with composure—has hindered us from resolutely walking in Yah's purpose for our lives. Not only are emotions indicators of what dwells in our hearts (Luke 6:45), but if not mastered, they will lead us to death (Prov. 16:25). On Tuesday, July 12, 2016, at 4:30 p.m., this truth would be solidified in my life as I stepped into Yah's mission for me to emotionally liberate the lives of boys and men.

The Cave of Adullam

I founded the Cave of Adullam Transformational Training Academy (CATTA), or "the Cave," in 2008 after realizing that boys were in dire need of Emotional Stability Training. Our mission is to teach, train, and transform boys into comprehensive men of the Most High. Men who are physically conscious, mentally astute, and spiritually strong enough to navigate through the pressures of this world without succumbing to their negative emotions.

When I first started the CATTA, there were many "Scared Straight" programs in Michigan, and I had even participated in a couple. However, I quickly discovered that inflicting trauma will never help a boy release it but instead teach him to suppress it. Aggressively yelling at an angry, fatherless boy is like attempting to stitch up a wound with a needle but no thread. Nowadays, you'll be hard-pressed to find a Scared Straight program because discipline without love is ineffectual. Our boys need to be healed, not scared straight.

One evening, Bruce, one of my eight-year-old recruits in the Cave, was taking his initiation test to proceed to rite-of-passage training. I had ceased videoing our recruits' initiation tests by that point, but this evening I wanted to record this moment for Bruce's father, my friend Bruce Collins II. I had to set up the camera quickly because it was a last-minute thought. Had I known that video would go viral and be viewed more than 100 million times, deeply impacting people of all ethnicities worldwide, I would have at least taken time to focus the lens.

What those millions of viewers did not know was that months prior to Bruce's initiation test, he had expressed that he wanted to quit the CATTA because he was nervous about failing his test. He wasn't the first recruit to feel this way and will not be the last. This is why we attach key life and biblical principles to all of our teachings. Bruce had no idea that the board he had to break to complete his initiation would represent his greatest barrier: a fear of failure. Thankfully, his loving and faithful father encouraged him to continue training.

So here was eight-year-old Bruce that evening, nervous yet willing to take his initiation test. His mother and father were there to support him. His family and fellow recruits, referred to in the CATTA as "cave brothers," were watching intensely. He struggled through his emotions and successfully passed the initiation's spiritual component. The next part, the physical component, wasn't as mentally demanding. Everyone in the academy, including Bruce, knew he should pass it with ease because he had practiced for weeks. And the board he struggled to break was the one board he had broken repeatedly weeks prior while practicing for his initiation test. He now only needed to execute, from a set position, the proper form of a thrust punch and a knee strike while repeatedly breaking a board. However, to Bruce's surprise, this same board became like an emotional barrier or, should I say, like a prison wall.

From childhood, emotional barriers arise when we experience failure, embarrassment, and rejection, just to name a few. However, we erect some of these barriers on our own in hopes of protecting our hearts from any more painful experiences. These same prison walls accompany countless boys into manhood, prohibiting them from becoming all they were created to be.

During our adolescent years, emotional barriers can be initiated by a school bully, academic challenges, fatherlessness, obesity, negative peer pressure, or emotional wounds from our mothers. Unfortunately, due to societal pressure to perform, when a boy becomes an adult, these same barriers become impenetrable walls. The school bully is now an intimidating coworker who stops you from going after an open position with higher pay than his. Although your weight is under control, the traumatic memory of being obese now prevents you from asking the woman of your dreams out for dinner. Fatherlessness or a mother wound has you seeking affirmation via pornography. Do you see how this all plays out?

Fear of looking bad or being perceived as a failure greatly hinders us from transforming our minds. Do not be deceived; this is rooted in false pride—a fear-based ego. I often say that mistakes are our greatest teachers. The only bad mistake is the one we didn't learn from. In my life, every time I have feared failure, I have failed.

This is why we emphasize during the initiation test that the board represents an emotional barrier blocking the recruit from resolutely walking in Yah's purpose for his life. For Bruce, it was a fear of failure. Because he hadn't trained enough internally to break emotional barriers, he succumbed to his fear when his external strength waned.

Bruce successfully executed his thrust punches with good form and broke the board swiftly with his right fist three times, but he only broke it once with his nondominant hand. Many believe that strength and power are the same. However, in the CATTA, we teach that strength depends on the physical ability of the body, but power is based on the spiritual rule *over* the body. This is what millions witnessed in 1997 when Michael Jordan overcame flu-like symptoms to win game five of the NBA finals against the Utah Jazz. When Jordan's physical strength could no longer

> **Strength depends on the physical ability of the body, but power is based on the spiritual rule *over* the body.**

endure the demand needed to lead his team to victory, he had to draw from the power within him to win.

In the CATTA, we call on a greater power from within, *Rūach Hä Kōdësh*, Hebrew for the Holy Spirit. The apostle Paul wrote that those who are servants of Yah are strengthened with power through His Holy Spirit in our bodies (Eph. 3:16).

What those outside of the CATTA do not see in any video of these initiation tests is what takes place inside when a recruit breaks the board. Don't be fooled by the physical act alone. Yes, breaking multiple boards without spaces between them takes physical striking power; however, recruits must first break the boards introspectively. I cannot count the times I've seen a recruit's negative thoughts or bad habits stop him from breaking a board in our academy.

We who follow the Most High are to have a renewed mind, not a negative one (Rom. 12:2). A mind that focuses its thoughts on whatever is good (Phil. 4:8). This is why I often tell my recruits that the fight must be won within before they can actually win; this is what I emphasized to Bruce during his initiation test. When he mentally grasped this principle, he physically broke the board!

Regrettably, countless men avoid the process it takes to become emotionally stable, and they remain in self-imposed emotional incarceration. There are many reasons for this, but the main one is our fear of being vulnerable. I often joke that a man would rather run through a burning building than sit with his thoughts and emotions. As platinum hip-hop artist Drake says, "I pop bottles 'cause I bottle my emotions."[2]

Unfortunately, suppression leads to depression. This is why it's imperative that we learn how to evaluate our emotions daily.

The more unresolved anger, anxiety, and distress we harbor in our hearts, the less capable we are of abundantly living in the present. When emotional issues go unaddressed, they become mental and behavioral issues. Case in point: Steve Stephens.

It was April 16, 2017—a beautiful afternoon for seventy-four-year-old Robert Godwin Sr. to walk outside after an Easter meal with his family in Cleveland, Ohio. Miles away, thirty-seven-year-old Steve Stephens, a children's mental health worker, was recording himself on a video to upload to Facebook. He expressed how he had a lot of "built-up anger and frustration" and was looking for random people to kill. Within minutes, Stephens was heard saying, "Found me somebody I'm about to kill . . . he a old dude."[3]

That innocent "old dude" was Mr. Godwin.

Stephens slowly pulled up, stopped his white Ford Fusion, and exited his car. He walked resolutely toward Mr. Godwin while asking, "Can you do me a favor?"

Surprised by the question, Mr. Godwin turned around suspiciously.

Stephens then asked Mr. Godwin to say his girlfriend's name, stressing, "She's the reason this is about to happen to you." According to later reports, Stephens and his girlfriend had recently ended their long-term relationship.

Stephens then abruptly pulled out a gun and shot Mr. Godwin at point-blank range. With no remorse, Stephens continued recording the video for his Facebook followers, even filming Mr. Godwin's body on the ground before walking back to his vehicle. Stephens then drove 103 miles to Erie, Pennsylvania, where he was recognized two days later by a McDonald's employee.

Police responded immediately to the sighting, but before the officers could apprehend Stephens, he pulled out his gun and shot himself inside his vehicle. This is just one of many tragic stories that emphasize the danger of suppressing our emotions. It's crucial that we learn how to sit still with our thoughts and feelings so we can express how we feel without losing self-control. In a world that condemns men for being transparent, bottling up our emotions may seem like the masculine thing to do. But it's not the wisest because when life shakes us and the pressure rises, our tops will pop. The mind can only bear so much before it breaks down.

The mind can only bear so much before it breaks down.

I receive countless messages through social media from men asking how to win this war within. Almost always, when I tell them to run toward the battle instead of away from it, they get disheartened and our communication goes cold. Let me be real with you, no war is ever won without a fight. On this journey to emotional freedom, you'll discover that the hardest part is not breaking free, but staying free.

And the best time to prepare for war is when there is peace. It's imperative that you learn how to process what you're feeling *before* your negative thoughts become toxic actions. You need to rule your emotions so you will maintain self-control. Do not be deceived: the same thoughts that imprisoned you will rise up again when you make a mistake, face a trial, get in an argument with your wife, or lose patience with your children.

Teaching you how to fight physically is one thing, but empowering you with the skills to rule your emotions is another. I've been training in martial arts for more than twenty-five years, and although I've seen the benefits of martial arts discipline, I've always been confounded about how a martial artist can make it to the level of a black belt in the dojo but remain a white belt in life. How can a man train for decades to fight one or two attackers with ease, yet is unable to mentally overcome a few stressors in his life? Anyone who is trained can break bricks or choke someone, and someone untrained can break a jaw, but what matters most is when you no longer have to hurt someone in order to prove you're powerful. The fight starts before you form your fist. Before you fire the bullets. Before you speak the words.

So, right now, sit up and get off the bed in your cell. Take a step toward the open door. If you are hesitant, that's okay, but do not sit back down. You've been through a lot, so be kind to yourself—no self-condemnation. The fact that you've made it this far in life and you've picked up this book confirms you haven't given up and are willing to take a journey inward. But you must complete your first training assignment before you move on to the next chapter.

Grab your journal or a pad of paper. Make a list of every area in your life in which you need to achieve victory. Beside each item on your list, write down any negative thoughts you have about each area and the emotions you need to express. Don't hold back. Write it all out just as you hear it in your head.

In doing so, you'll begin to learn how to effectively wage and win the war within.

In ancient Israel when there was a threat of war, the warriors would yell the Hebrew word *milchamah* (pronounced mil-khaw-maw), which means battle,[4] and run with all vigilance to defeat the approaching enemy. We shout this battle cry in the CATTA when we are preparing our minds and bodies for training.

So, after you've written out everything you can think of, yell with me, "Milchamah!" because the Enemy sees that you are escaping emotional incarceration. Even if you feel unsure as we get started here, instead of fretting, stay focused so that you can effectively wage and win the war that will change your life.

TWO

MISCONSTRUED MASCULINITY

Never trust a warrior who cannot cry.
—*Irish Proverb*

I flew to Washington, DC, a few years ago with one of my friends, who was a man of the Most High. Just before we took off, I turned to him and said, "Let's pray for a safe and comfortable flight." He smirked, "What? You scared?" His condescending tone came through loud and clear. I chuckled as I shook my head and began to pray by myself. He elbowed my arm and said, "Hey Jay, you're right. We should pray."

When men chide one another for appearing afraid, or when we admonish one another to "stay strong," we are subconsciously telling ourselves that something is wrong when we are fatigued or weak. It's as if we're reminding one another to keep up the masculine facade. However, men of the Most High know it's only in our weakness that the power of Yahushua is perfected (2 Cor. 12:9).

So, what does it mean to be masculine? The dictionary defines *masculine* as an adjective:

1. Pertaining to or characteristic of a man or men: [e.g.,] masculine attire
2. Having qualities traditionally ascribed to men, as strength and boldness[1]
   Synonyms include *virile, macho, manly, muscular, strong,* and *powerful.*[2]

Yet this adjective will never come close to defining the comprehensive nature with which Yah created man. Men are more complex than this. Is it any wonder that many of us struggle with our true identities? From early childhood and throughout life, we try to conform to a narrow definition of male essence. Being a male becomes a never-ending struggle to reach perfection, the pinnacle of bravery, fearlessness, and reserve. But this image of perfection is false and becomes the root problem in too many of our lives.

Equal Opportunity Emotions

Although women such as Harriet Tubman, Rosa Parks, and many female athletes have possessed masculine qualities, it is men who are pressured and confined to the limited definition of masculinity. Living as a human male becomes a relentless battle to only be the essence of strength and boldness. And when you don't feel brave or strong, you are shamed for not being a "real" man. The battle between your heart (who you really are) and your mind (who you think you should be) intensifies as you struggle to conform. Then you become emotionally imbalanced.

But it doesn't have to be that way. The truth is, Yah did not create some emotions for men and others for women. He created both genders human and all emotions for both genders!

Consider the biblical account of Deborah and Barak. Deborah was a prophet as well as a judge who settled disputes between the Israelites. Barak was the military commander whose name meant "lightning."

These two individuals lived at a time when the nation's disobedience to Yah brought about the Canaanites' oppressive rule over the Israelites for twenty years. One day the Most High told Deborah to summon Barak and tell him that the Most High was commanding him to assemble ten thousand men of Israel to go and fight the Canaanite army. If Barak obeyed, Yah promised that Israel would be victorious.

> **Yah did not create some emotions for men and others for women. He created both genders human and all emotions for both genders!**

Although Barak was a warrior, he lacked courage in that milestone moment. He told Deborah, "If you will go with me, then I will go; but if you will not go with me, I will not go" (Judg. 4:8). Deborah agreed to accompany Barak but told him that, since he would not go as Yah commanded, the honor for the battle would be given to a woman. Then Deborah arose courageously and went with Barak to fight the Canaanite army. As promised, the Most High gave Israel a great victory that day.

Many men downplay Barak's fear as simply a lack of faith in Yah. But let's look at this in context. Although Barak led an army of ten thousand men, the Canaanite army had the distinct advantage of nine hundred iron chariots—considered by historians as tanks of that day. Barak feared this moment so much that he was not only willing to be the first commander to take a woman with him to war, but he didn't think twice about Deborah being given all the honor.

Barak was scared. And through his actions, or lack thereof, he admitted it to himself and to Deborah. Which I, personally, find commendable. For all we know, it may have taken more courage for him to admit his fear than it would have to head into battle without Deborah. As men, we have a choice when fear arises. We can either be courageous enough to tell the truth, or we can risk dire consequences by pretending we're not afraid.

My heart grieves every time I think of the teenagers in my city who died young because they refused to listen to what the emotion of fear was telling them. One fourteen-year-old young man I mentored briefly told his close friend that he knew if he went to a certain party, there would be trouble. A group of guys there who were jealous of him had threatened to kill him. Instead of acknowledging his fear and staying away, he chose to suppress it and go to the party. He wanted to prevent any rumors spreading that he was scared. He was more afraid of being seen as a coward than of being murdered. Tragically, that was the last party he would ever attend. He was shot and killed that night.

We cannot afford to be deceived by our egos. Oftentimes, we think we are being courageous, but in actuality, we're reacting unwisely due to our fear of looking bad or failing. If boys and men today were encouraged to feel fear instead of being pressured to follow the masculine mandate (a cultural order that coerces men to only be masculine), they would make choices that would help them live fuller, longer lives. Former South African president and anti-apartheid activist Nelson Mandela once said, "The brave man is not he who does not feel afraid, but he who conquers that fear."[3] So when we think about bravery, or courage, we can think about it in terms of taking the right action despite the fear we feel.

Now let's go back to the story of Barak. Was his fear simply a lack of faith? Do not be deceived; a lack of courage is actually a lack of personal confidence, not a lack of faith in Yah. That's why, when Israel's leader from generations before, Joshua, was afraid, Yah didn't tell him to have faith. He told Joshua three times to be strong and courageous (Josh. 1:1–9). Joshua knew who Yah was; he just didn't know who *he* was in that moment. Clearly, Barak knew who he was, which allowed him to feel fear rather than to fake it, because going into a war without courage could have cost him his life, not to mention Israel's freedom.

As long as men stay in the box of masculinity, we will never be able to navigate through our emotions and win the war within. Moses, Joshua, Gideon, and other mighty men of the Most High waged this same internal war when they initially feared being obedient to Yah's command. The keyword is *initially*. When we are able to access and feel the gamut of emotions the Most High created in us, we are liberated not only to feel fear and make better decisions in the midst of adversity but also to rule any negative thought that could stop us from conquering timidity!

More Than Masculine

In 2010, my beloved mother began showing signs of dementia, and her symptoms got worse every week. My heart felt crushed and my soul became anxious because the first love of my life was deteriorating before my eyes. At the time, I didn't know how to express my grief. I only knew how to be strong and provide solutions for every situation. Nicole and I purchased a ranch-style home with an in-law suite so Mom could live with us, and I spent countless hours renovating—until dementia threw us a curveball. My mother's geropsychology doctor called one day to inform us that her dementia was accelerating so much that she would need twenty-four-hour care from a professional caregiver.

My mom did not have good health insurance, and her only income was from social security and a small pension from her previous marriage. At the time, I was barely making enough to give my family a comfortable lifestyle. The pressure and emotional pain I felt from not being able to provide the care I desired for my mother was heart-rending, but I did not know how to express my feelings.

So, instead of crying to release the stress or sharing my true feelings with Nicole, I leaned on the only emotion I felt comfortable expressing: anger. I snapped at Nicole for suggesting that we start looking for a place for Mom before she became more aggressive than we could handle.

"There's no way I'm putting my mother in a nursing home!" I asserted adamantly.

Although I could have won an Oscar for playing the role of a commander going to battle, Nicole's calm response confirmed she knew I was scared. "Let's pray, Jay."

We held each other's hands and asked the Most High for help.

That night I decided to sit on our deck to pray and meditate. Within minutes, Yah's Holy Spirit spoke to my heart: "Jason, there's no way you will be able to give your mother the care she needs if you're only being a masculine male. To give her the quality of life you desire for her, you must now become a *comprehensive* man." But what did that mean?

A comprehensive man is courageous but also compassionate, strong but sensitive. A man who lives freely from the good in his heart and not his fears. A comprehensive man embraces all of his emotions so he can express them rather than be ruled by them. In contrast, a masculine male only allows himself to feel and exude emotions that are culturally acceptable for men. These were all things I would come to learn and understand more fully in time, but it was in that pivotal moment when I first heard this distinction between the two that I started my journey from emotional incarceration to living wholeheartedly as the man Yah created me to be.

In the weeks and months ahead, my journey toward comprehensive manhood accelerated as my mother's mental health declined. The day after Yah's Holy Spirit spoke to me, we received a call from our friend Kourtney, who informed us about an assisted living home just two minutes from our new house. The owner and caregiver had taken great care of our pastor's father and had recently opened her home for women—and she had an open bed. Nicole and I eagerly set up an appointment. The home was beautiful, and the owner, Kathy, was a godsend. She worked with our budget, and Mom felt at home . . . for an hour.

A comprehensive man embraces all of his emotions so he can express them rather than be ruled by them.

A few hours after we left, I received a call from Kathy stating that my mother was destroying things. Nicole and I immediately raced back to Kathy's house. As I pulled up, I noticed the living room window protruding like a special effect in a blockbuster movie. My mother had thrown a large plant at the window. Praise Yah it didn't shatter.

Mom's dementia made her paranoid, which caused her to relive the unresolved trauma she had experienced in her past. Everyone became a threat, including me. She would yell at her roommates and fight physically with them. For the first two years she was in that home, I would allow my two dominant emotions—frustration and anger—to surface at will, but they eventually rendered themselves useless for such a heartwrenching trial. I quickly discovered that I would have to learn how to express my emotions differently in order to bring calm to chaos.

One day in anger, I pleaded for the Most High to take my mother's life. I believed she was no longer living, just tortured by her own thoughts. In a calm voice, Yah responded, "Jason, that's not love; that's fear. Remember, you must become a comprehensive man. Live from the good in your heart, not your fears."

I often say I may not know what works, but I know what doesn't work. Since I am a man of principles, I shifted my perspective and prayed that Yah would allow me to see this distressing situation with His eyes, so I could learn what love truly was. And He answered my prayer.

I created a concept called the "dementia roller coaster." When I got on it with my mother, I would always be unstable emotionally, up and down, bouncing between anxiety and fear. So, when Mom got on the coaster, I made sure I stayed on solid ground. Like a caring parent, I would wait patiently until she reached the end of the ride, then I would calmly reach out to hold her hand and help her catch her mental balance.

One day I received an alarming call that my mother had experienced another transient ischemic attack (TIA, a mini-stroke). I rushed to Kathy's house to ride with Mom to the hospital.

After the doctors stabilized her, I walked into the bathroom and cried out to Yah. "Please heal my mother. I don't want her to go now."

Like a proud father, Yah responded, "Now you've got it! This is love. This is living from the good in your heart and not your fears (1 John 4:18). You are a comprehensive man."

Thankfully, my mother recovered faster than before, and this time the rehabilitation journey was an experience I wouldn't trade for anything. For weeks afterward, every time I went to see her, I combed her hair, filed her fingernails, massaged her scalp to calm her mind, and rubbed her feet to relax her body.

Warm tears now soak my face as I type this because I am so thankful that I boldly waged and won this battle. Escaping from emotional incarceration liberated my heart. I always longed for an affectionate relationship with my mother, but the fear of being called a "momma's boy" made me restrain that emotion. It wasn't until I moved beyond the limitations of masculinity, that I was finally able to freely love her like I desired and she deserved.

As men of the Most High, when we only live through our masculine attributes, we can never do *all things* through Christ.

When He needs us to be patient, we can't.

When He needs us to be nurturing, we can't.

When He needs us to be compassionate, we can't.

And when He needs us to be weak so that His power is perfected, we can't (2 Cor. 12:9).

We are so much more than *priests*, *providers*, and *protectors*. This popular Christian alliteration used to motivate us actually puts tremendous pressure on us to perform. And when we grow weary of living a performance-based life, we have nothing left with which to love ourselves and our families. Yah *created* us to be comprehensive! No longer should we fear being rejected or shamed for being kindhearted, compassionate, or, dare I say, nurturing.

We Are Also Nurturers!

Fathers are rarely viewed as the nurturing parent, if at all. But after the tragic passing of Kobe Bryant and his daughter Gianna in a helicopter crash, pictures surfaced online of Kobe freely operating as a nurturer. Men across the globe began sharing images of themselves nurturing their daughters along with #girldad, which trended for weeks on social media. Men have always been nurturers, but sadly, most of us only feel safe allowing that expression of love to be displayed through protection and provision.

I will never forget the time my son, Jason, had to have surgery on his ear. After the surgery, my wife and I patiently sat in the post-surgery waiting room until it was time to see Jason. Suddenly, we heard a familiar yell coming from Jason's room. He had just awakened from the anesthesia and was scared. Within seconds, one of the nurses came out and requested that Nicole come back to calm Jason down.

Although I was offended that I wasn't asked to tend to my son as well, I checked my emotions because Nicole is a registered nurse. I knew she could assess the situation and comfort Jason. But then Jason yelled again. I calmly but resolutely walked over to the receptionist desk and told the nurse that I needed to check on my son. She tried to convince me that everything was okay, but my silence and steady stare motivated her to open the door. To the staff's amazement, my presence and words calmed Jason's soul almost immediately.

My son knows I am a protector and a provider, but he loves that I am also a nurturer like many other good fathers. It's not only okay for men to love our children in this way, it's long overdue.

Freedom of Self-Expression

A comprehensive man is not ashamed to admit what he enjoys in the world. I've always loved flowers, but for many years I would only buy them for my wife because it wasn't considered masculine for me to want flowers for myself. As a student of many martial arts, I was intrigued when I discovered that some of the greatest warriors had an affinity for flowers. One evening before the end of *Iaido* (Japanese sword) class, our teacher informed us that the Zen art of *ikebana* (flower arranging) was traditionally practiced by the samurai, even the great Miyamoto Musashi—an undefeated samurai renowned for his swordsmanship.

Ikebana offers a ritualistic but starkly personal form of self-expression in which the arranger creates beauty with colors taken from the palette of life. This contemplative and slow practice offered the highly skilled samurai warriors a form of emotional balance. Studies reveal that simply being in the presence of flowers elevates mood, measurably increases feelings of life satisfaction, and decreases depression and anxiety while promoting positive social behavior.[4] The samurai warriors of medieval and early modern Japan must have known something many of us don't. They were very fond of *sakura* flowers (cherry blossoms)—and *no one* dared to insult their manhood.

Now that I'm free from emotional incarceration, I confidently peruse flowers at the market and select the ones that elicit the feelings I desire. You may not be fond of flowers like I am, but when you allow yourself the freedom to feel what you feel without shame, you might be surprised at what arises. You might realize that you have an affinity for a different genre of music or art, or maybe a sport other than basketball.

I encourage you to challenge the status quo—to begin again and reach further—and break free from misconstrued masculinity so you can embrace your humanity. You were fearfully and wonderfully made, inside and out (Ps. 139:14).

Masculinity and Your Health

It's no secret that men do not like going to the doctor. In a recent study by the Cleveland Clinic, 72 percent of men said they would rather do household chores than go to the doctor. Almost two-thirds (65 percent) said they avoid going to the doctor as long as possible, and 37 percent said they've withheld information from their doctors so they wouldn't have to deal with the potential diagnosis.[5] Ironically, it's the fear of dying that leads us to early graves, and our unwillingness to express it or be vulnerable will continue to take us out.

Approximately 191,000 men in the United States are diagnosed with prostate cancer annually, which is the second-leading cause of cancer death in men in the United States.[6] The main test used to detect prostate cancer is called a PSA (prostate-specific antigen), and the majority of men are cool with taking it because it's "noninvasive." Just a quick skin prick and a few vials of blood, and you're done.

Unfortunately, some men can still have prostate cancer with normal PSA levels. Which is why I also have my doctor administer the hypermasculine male's kryptonite: the digital rectal examination (DRE). This exam literally takes less than ten seconds, but many men would rather fall on their swords than have a doctor insert a finger up their rectums.

I often have to exude a ton of effort to persuade my friends to have their prostates examined. By their resistance, you'd think all of our masculinity is removed by the time the doctor has taken off his rubber glove. And having tissue handed to us with which to clean ourselves is like a nail in the coffin of manliness. This mentality and false definition of manhood is literally killing us.

No one can be strong all the time. If you continue to allow your life to be defined by one adjective—*masculine*—you soon may not have a life. It's time for you to start the process of becoming who you are really meant to be: a comprehensive man. Please do not misconstrue what I am saying. Masculinity itself is not toxic. However, a man can become toxic when he allows his humanity to only be defined by masculinity.

Consider the American pit bull terrier, for example. For decades, this dog was bred to be a protector and fighter. The traumatic and sometimes torturous training eventually caused this beautiful breed to become unstable and volatile, even banned in many cities. If not for the relentless efforts of dog-rescue initiatives, the masses would have never known that the American pit bull terrier is also capable of being a loving, compassionate companion and family dog.

Speaking of dogs, I once shared with a newly acquainted friend that I was considering buying a dog.

"I love dogs!" he exclaimed. "What kind do you want?"

"A cavapoo, Cavalier King Charles spaniel and poodle mix," I replied.

Perplexed, he yelled, "Brother, you need a man dog! Like a rottweiler, a German shepherd, or a bullmastiff!"

I wanted to ask what qualified those breeds as "man dogs," because I've raised two of those breeds and didn't feel more of a man than I do now. But I had a feeling he wasn't ready to receive the information that the poodle is historically an efficient hunter and, when bred with the Cavalier King Charles spaniel, becomes the ultimate gentleman's dog.

Do you see it now? When we allow our lives to be imprisoned by one adjective (masculine), we limit our lives and never truly live up to Yah's comprehensive definition of a man.

Before you move on to the next chapter, you must complete your next training assignment. First, identify someone in your life who needs your care. Someone you love but sometimes avoid due to the non-masculine emotions that arise when you're around this person. This can be a parent, grandparent, aging relative, child, or even your wife. Allow your actions to express the suppressed love you have for this person, and wage war against every emotion that tries to stop you from attaining freedom. For example, my father was absent throughout my entire childhood; however, after he began suffering from the effects of Parkinson's disease, I pushed through the years of emotional pain to be by his side when he needed me the most. During a visit with my father one afternoon, the Most High told me to say, "Dad, thank you for being a great father."

This didn't make sense to me until I saw how this act of love freed my father to cry and finally say, "I love you, son."

I waged war against every emotion that could have stopped me from attaining what I longed for. Now it's your turn. Do this exercise until it becomes a natural expression of who you are. I forewarn you, as with any war, sacrifice will be needed to win. Therefore, it's crucial that you understand what sacrifice really is, so that you don't give up when the battle gets difficult.

Sacrifice is not necessarily doing what you want to do but doing what you *don't* want to do that needs to be done. The night Yahushua was betrayed by Judas and arrested by the officers of the temple guard, He prayed for the Most High to take the cup of sacrifice from Him (Matt. 26:39). This is a real moment that we all will face. When our desires betray us and our negative emotions attempt to arrest our purpose, we must rule our emotions so that we will respond the way Yahushua did to Yah: "Not My will, but Yours be done."

You must be broken before you can become whole.

This is a defining moment in your training to wage the war within. Embrace it. You must be broken before you can become whole because pride still goes before destruction and a haughty spirit before a fall (Prov. 16:18). The life you long for is before you, but the guards (your fears) have sounded the alarm, and they do not want you to escape. So with all vigilance, fight to feel, and yell with me, "Milchamah!" The war has begun.

THREE

PUTTING PEACE IN PERSPECTIVE

Sometimes God calms the storm,
but sometimes God lets the storm
rage and calms His child.
—LESLIE GOULD, *THE AMISH NANNY*

One day after I facilitated an orientation for the CATTA at a high school in Detroit, I noticed one of the students running out of the men's bathroom as I was walking down the hall. I recognized him as a ninth grader who had shown interest in training with me. He had an impressionable personality, and although I could tell he desired to do good, like many boys his age, he struggled with succumbing to negative peer pressure.

I stopped him and asked, "What's going on in the bathroom?"

He froze and stared at me for a moment, then responded

hesitantly, "They're bullying someone in there." I appreciated his honesty and watched him run off.

When I walked into the bathroom, I discovered five young men surrounding a disabled boy who stood trembling, supported only with a forearm crutch on his left arm. I closed the door behind me and faced the boys. The first emotion to arise in me was indignation. I have a deep enmity toward bullying, and it made me angry to see a vulnerable kid being treated unfairly.

But instead of reacting by yelling and berating like some of their teachers would—or slamming one of them against the wall like I've seen security guards do in the past—I paused and allowed my silence to set the tone before I spoke. I knew I had to rule my emotions because I didn't want to hurt them, nor could I tell if any of them had weapons. I leaned back against the door, and the peace that passes all understanding rose up in place of my anger, allowing me to access wisdom.

"If you were me, and that was my son," I began, "what would you do right now?"

They all looked like they had seen a ghost. Again, I allowed the power of silence to stimulate their thoughts and intently stared each one of them in their eyes as if I were looking through them. At the time, I was a chiseled six feet one with 230 pounds of muscle, so when I began to walk toward them, they quickly parted like the Red Sea and ran out the door. I then helped the disabled boy out of the bathroom and made sure he was safe as he made his way to his next class.

I could have easily allowed my anger to rule—or ruin—that moment, but because I have a practice that brings me the peace of Yah in any circumstance, I was able to navigate through my emotions and dexterously defuse the situation. I gave those boys a way out of their heartless intentions by using the power of words instead of physical force. As a result, three of them came back later and apologized. Although my appearance can be intimidating to some, all of the boys I work with will tell you it's my resolute spirit that gains their respect.

Mark Twain is often attributed as having said, "It's not the size of the dog in the fight, it's the size of the fight in the dog." A man can be powerful regardless of his stature. But he must display the will needed to win a fight or bring calm to a volatile situation.

Emotional Emancipation

Most people think of peace as an absence of trouble—a utopian, quiet kind of place. But we must cast away this limited understanding of peace if we're actually going to experience it. Peace is not a place; it's a state of mind that *releases* negative thoughts, *reflects* on what's good, and *resets* so that it stays focused on Yah. Peace has to be *in us* before it can be around us.

Peace has to be *in us* before it can be around us.

Many of us often ask the Most High to give us peace, but we expect Him to make our circumstances better in order for us to experience it. We miss the truth that the reason His peace passes all understanding is not because our situations improve but because we cast our cares on Him and shift our focus onto the things that are good (Phil. 4:6–8).

Even if you're not a man of the Most High, you will still greatly benefit from changing your perspective of peace and gaining the biblical understanding needed to maintain rule over your emotions. Trust me, if you continue to make peace a place, you will only be able to attain it when you are in a particular location or circumstance instead of maintaining it wherever you are.

One afternoon before class began in the CATTA, all of my recruits complained that they were tired from being at school all day. I always allow a safe space for them to express their emotions, but it was imperative that I take advantage of this moment. This class would be the hardest they would experience since enrolling. We trained relentlessly that afternoon, and it was amazing to see their fiery spirits push through their perceived fatigue.

I shouted, "Are you tired now?"

In unison they responded, "No, sir!"

With a smile on my face, I asked, "When is the best time to be tired?"

They all stared at me, baffled, then one of them answered, "When it's time for bed, sir."

I proudly affirmed him, "Exactly, my son!" When we allow an emotion to influence our physiological state in the wrong moment, not only does peace escape us, but stress constricts our progress.

For us to be able to command peace in any situation, we must learn how to wean our souls from the cares of this world so we can walk by Yah's Holy Spirit. When we allow

His words, thoughts, plans, and purposes to fill every part of our lives, we are able to maintain the peace needed to reign over the chaos of our day-to-day battles. But to do this, first we must face the real problem: our uncontrolled souls. In other words, our desires that oppose the will of Yah for our lives. This is why it's imperative that we wage the war within *daily*—quieting and stilling our souls so that we can boldly walk by the Spirit of Yah instead of being led astray by our emotions (Ps. 131:2).

We've all seen the cartoon where the good and bad angels stand on the shoulders of a man trying to make a decision. This is a perfect illustration of the introspective war, the battle between our souls and Yah's Holy Spirit. The Scriptures also speak of this war constantly taking place inside all of us (Rom. 2:15). Whether you believe in the Most High or not, we all experience it.

Should I apologize to my wife or keep arguing with her?
Should I have a meeting with my boss to share my concerns or quit my job?
Should I deescalate the situation or knock this [expletive] out?

Before I surrendered my life to the Most High and received His Holy Spirit to help me navigate through my negative emotions, I would, without hesitation, pick the latter option in all three scenarios. The soul will always try to hinder you from walking and fighting by the Spirit. But when we have received Yah's Spirit, we have an inner "referee" who will blow the whistle before we make a foul. That doesn't mean things get easy, though. Even after becoming a new creation in Christ, I still have to fight to subdue my soul.

The Spirit says, "Be still," but the soul says, "Worry."

I was for a long time what you would call a "soulish" Christian, a follower of Yahushua who was a slave to my desires instead of being obedient to Yah's will. On the exterior you saw a smile, but inside I was a miserable man. And like the apostle Paul, I didn't really understand myself. I wanted to do what was right, but instead I did what I hated (Rom. 7:15). There's nothing worse than being the bad guy when you desire to be a good man.

I was a slave to my emotionally erratic soul. I had become very passive aggressive, indirectly expressing my toxic emotions instead of articulating them with courageous transparency and composure. I did not know how to renew my mind; I was unable to release negative emotions. And so I had little to no capacity for tolerance, peace, or joy in my life. This not only hindered me greatly from surrendering to Yah's will but also kept me from experiencing sustained periods of peace, even when the world around me was calm.

And when things weren't calm, I would blame everything on the devil instead of placing blame on what he used to get the best of me—my emotions. The soul is the seat of our emotions—influencing our thoughts, passions, desires, and actions—and can be easily shaken when adversity comes. This is why it's crucial that we change our perspective of peace. This life will never be absent of "storms." Nor should we despise them when they come.

These storms aren't meant to destroy us, but to define us. They are opportunities for spiritual training and growth.

Without the troubles we encounter in this world, we will continue to search for an escape from them instead of finding peace in Him. As one of my mentors, Jimmie Davis Compton Jr., penned, "When your perception of God is larger than your perception of the storm you're in, you can remain calm and even call good times to rise and come forth."[1]

Peace + Storm = Peace

From the effects of global warming and widespread violence to racial injustice and the COVID-19 pandemic, our lives these days more often look like a ship tossed to and fro by the waves at sea than a canoe floating on a placid lake. Many of us struggle with maintaining peace in the midst of all this due to our desire to stay in control or stay comfortable. I, too, struggled with the illusion of control, even after surrendering my life to the Most High. For years I fought to have power over situations that I actually could not influence.

Thankfully, I eventually realized that the only things I could control were my thoughts and emotions, which ultimately determine the way I respond to life's pressures. When I made this mental shift, I was able to embrace the biblical truth that I was not created to live a stress-free life but to be a light in this dark world (Matt. 5:14–16). After fervently praying for Yah's perspective of peace, He answered me with this passage of Scripture:

And a great windstorm arose, and the waves beat into the boat, so that it was already filling. But He [Yahushua] was in

the stern, asleep on a pillow. And they [the disciples] awoke
Him and said to Him, "Teacher, do You not care that we are
perishing?" Then He arose and rebuked the wind, and said
to the sea, "Peace, be still!" And the wind ceased and there
was a great calm. (Mark 4:37–39 NKJV)

I've heard this passage of Scripture taught many times, but
it wasn't until I was in the midst of my own storm that I was
able to grasp what Yahushua was trying to teach the disciples.
Let's take a deeper look at the ending of this passage.

Yahushua said to the storm, "Peace, be still." In the natural sense, He simply said, "Be quiet." But in the spiritual
sense, when I meditated on how one could sleep through
a life-threatening situation, my own perspective of peace
changed.

Let's say you adopted a rescue dog named Max. You and
your children were told by the shelter that, due to years of being
abused by his previous owner, Max at times would randomly
run throughout the house with a sense of urgency. One night
while you were sleeping, Max woke with the memories of being
abused and started running recklessly throughout your home.
Since you knew his actions were not due to a burglar seeking
entrance into your house, you went back to sleep. However,
your children became frightened and raced into your room to
wake you up. In this scenario, you might rise calmly, walk into
the living room, and say, "Max, be still."

What if when Yahushua said to the storm, "Peace, be still,"
He was literally calling the storm by the name of *Peace*? Could
He have been teaching us that the turbulent storm was "peace
in motion"? Maybe to Yahushua, peace was simply moving.

Warrior, please understand, if this life were meant to be comfortable at all times, Yahushua would not have sent the Comforter (Holy Spirit). And when the Most High's Spirit dwells in us, and we focus on Him in times of trouble, we can experience His perfect peace and feel blessed even when we're stressed (Isa. 26:3).

Reflect, Release, Reset, Rest

It's common to believe that the mind controls the body, but as I mentioned, the soul is the seat of our emotions, which often overrule what the mind transmits. If we do not rule our soul, we lose self-control and become slaves to our emotions. Progress during the day and rest at night elude us.

As men, we often stay up at night because we haven't released the stress or disappointments of the day; this is why we must learn and apply what I call the four Rs:

- Reflect
- Release
- Reset
- Rest

If you want to experience peace, start and end each day with a moment to *reflect* on the turbulent things that have shaken your soul. Then, through prayer and meditation, allow your soul to *release* the cares of this world to the Most High so you can *reset*. Once your soul is stilled, you can experience *rest*—a byproduct of Yah's peace (Ps. 127:2).

To deepen this practice, I created a type of biblical meditation, which I call Shalach (pronounced shä-lakh'). *Shalach* is a Hebrew word that means to send, let go, or cast away.[2] It's active. In that sense, it is not a form of concentration, nor a New Age emptying of your mind. In Shalach meditation, the end goal is to eventually maintain a meditative state while moving, regardless of the stress or situation. My reasoning is that, if I have to sit still to meditate, how useful will it be during my day when I can't sit still but need Shalach's benefits the most?

To wage and win the war within, we must be able to "shalach" the stress of this world, whether we're lying down, sitting up, standing, walking, or even fighting. In the CATTA, when we drill techniques or spar, I command our recruits to maintain Shalach so they can keep their souls still regardless of the pressure of the attack coming their way.

The great warrior David said it best when he faced adversity: "I have composed and quieted my soul; like a weaned child rests against his mother, my soul is like a weaned child within me" (Ps. 131:2).

During one class, I saw my CATTA recruit Brayden struggling with anxiety during a club attack drill (when someone swings a stick at your head). So, I took over from my assistant who was teaching him. Even though I swung the padded stick slowly at Brayden's head, he flinched in fear.

"Relax," I said. "Nothing has happened yet, son . . . breathe. If you respond on a what-if, you'll get in trouble. You have to wait sometimes before you make that decision."

Because his emotions were ruling him, Brayden could only

focus on the padded stick instead of the real problem, the person swinging it.

When we are "soulish," we react erratically to every apparent threat instead of maintaining our peace and responding in a way that keeps us in an advantageous position. However, when we are able to shalach, we will never be threatened by the *appearance* of a threat. Within seconds of grasping this concept, Brayden began to move without anxiety, and I could fully swing the club at his head without fear of him moving prematurely and thus resulting in my striking my beloved recruit.

I find great joy in seeing these young men grow like this. Due in large part to our practice of Shalach in the CATTA, our evaluations show that 81 percent of our boys improve their grade point average by one letter grade *without tutoring*. When a man learns how to rule his emotions in any environment (school, work, war, etc.), he is able to perform at a higher capacity.

I realize that many Western Christians resist any form of meditation because they've heard that a person must "empty" themselves during such a practice. First, let me assure you that you cannot empty yourself of the Holy Spirit. The Bible testifies that He will never leave you (John 14:16). And second, when I mention emptying the self, I am referring to casting the cares of our souls on the Most High (Ps. 55:22). When we allow the soul to release the emotions that weigh us down, our vessels will momentarily become empty of the cares of this world, and we will be more capable of hearing the still small voice of Yah.

Outlining Shalach Meditation

I practice Shalach meditation daily so that I am able to access peace in any given moment. The inspiration for this practice of biblical meditation came to me from the prophet Elijah's struggle with depression in the cave and his subsequent moment with the Most High.

> And, behold, the LORD passed by, and a great and strong wind rent the mountains, and brake in pieces the rocks before the LORD; but the LORD was not in the wind: and after the wind an earthquake; but the LORD was not in the earthquake: And after the earthquake a fire; but the LORD was not in the fire: and after the fire a still small voice. (1 Kings 19:11–12 KJV)

Why was Elijah hiding in a cave? He had just killed 450 prophets of Jezebel, a wicked queen who murdered prophets of the Most High (1 Kings 18:22). After hearing what Elijah had done, Jezebel sent a threatening message to Elijah: "You killed my prophets. Now I'm going to kill you!" (1 Kings 19:1–2 CEV). Elijah was still a powerful prophet, but the weariness of fighting alone had taken a toll.

Uncast cares can make us look at life with our eyes and lean on our own understanding instead of leaning on the God who will help us overcome every trial we face. So let's take a cue from Elijah's encounter with Yah here. The following is an outline of how to practice Shalach meditation. I invite you to use it to access the peace you need daily.

Before we get started, make sure you have a pen and pad

next to you in case you feel led to write down the emotions you experience and what triggered those feelings. Also, if you're fortunate enough to hear from Yah, you won't want to miss the opportunity to write down what He says. Do not put parameters on this process. This is not a seven-step program to happiness. There is no time limit for each stage. Some cares take more effort to cast away, so please be patient with yourself.

Start off in a not-so-comfortable seated position. Why? Most meditation practices encourage people to sit in comfortable positions, but our purpose here is to wean the soul of its ways so we will one day live by the spirit. Sitting in a moderately uncomfortable position may cause the soul to complain, but this "struggle" cultivates an awareness of the perfect conflict between soul and spirit (Gal. 5:17). Also, breathing and prayer are very important elements of Shalach. When you inhale, focus on expanding your stomach instead of shallowly breathing through your chest—inhaling deeply through your mouth with your lips pursed. When you can no longer intake oxygen, hold your breath for three seconds, then exhale slowly from your mouth as long as possible. As we proceed through the stages, I will prompt you when to pray but please do not forget to breathe throughout.

Let's begin.

Stage One: The Winds of Worry

"And, behold, the LORD passed by, and a great and strong wind rent the mountains, and brake in pieces the rocks before the LORD; *but the* LORD *was not in the wind*" (1 Kings 19:11 KJV, emphasis added).

In this stage, you may feel as if the winds of worry are shaking your soul. Regardless of how you feel, please be still. Do not move from your seated position. Find comfort in knowing that what caused the wind to rent the mountains and break the rocks into pieces was the presence of the Most High as He passed by. You are not alone.

Stage Two: The Earthquake

"And after the wind an *earthquake, but the* LORD *was not in the earthquake*" (v. 11, emphasis added).

Sitting still through stressful thoughts and anxious feelings may become overwhelming, which could cause your soul to shake during this stage. Just as an earth tremor is a physical sign of what's going on beneath the earth's crust, an emotional tremor is a sign of what's going on inside of you. You may feel restlessness, irritability, and/or weariness. As you continue to work through these tremors, your soul may start to tell you this is too much to endure and you should stop and lie down. When this happens, boldly say to your soul, "I will not surrender to you. I am a warrior, and this war within must be waged!"

Stage Three: The Fire

"After the earthquake [there was] a fire, but the LORD was not in the fire" (v. 12).

This stage will take you through the heart-wrenching and *root* issues that shake your soul and compromise your peace, such as the loss of a loved one, marital discord, or sickness. You may begin to feel emotionally overwhelmed, but instead, raise a battle cry to the Most High for His peace during these moments. Again, your soul will try to arise and stop you from proceeding, but you must push through. Pray with me now:

*Abba (Father) Yah! You are a warrior God, so please
teach me how to wage and win this war. I'm tired
of losing to enemies within me; I now only want to
surrender to Your Spirit. Please give me the strength to
overcome all that I face.*

One by one, shalach your cares until they no longer consume you. Then embrace silence while breathing strong with the expectation of hearing from Yah.

Stage Four: The Still Small Voice of the Lord

"And after the fire [came] a *still small voice*" (v. 12 KJV, emphasis added).

The Most High cannot pour into our cups if we keep moving them. If the prophet Elijah had not been patient in stillness, he never would have heard the voice of the Most High. How often do we allow our restless minds, physical fatigue, or multitask-driven lives to dictate our time in meditation and prayer? I believe many of us struggle to hear from Yah because we make our requests known to Him but do not remain still long enough to hear His response. We want a genie at our command, not a sovereign God. Could you imagine having a child who would come to you and plead for financial provision or advice but immediately leave your presence after making his request? That's what we do to Yah every time we pray and do not allow Him a moment to respond. To hear His voice, we must desire it. True relationship with the Most High includes two-way conversations.

While breathing, listen intently throughout this stage. You may cry or again become overwhelmed with emotions—that's okay. Continue to sit still, breathe, and receive. Gradually, your soul will become quiet, and surely Yah will speak. If Yah tells you to write while He's talking, do so, but do not stop the breathing pattern. Like Elijah, once you've moved past the stages and have heard the still small voice of Yah, your soul will be settled.

If you did not hear Yah's voice, do not be discouraged. I don't hear His voice every time, but I feel His peace when I cast away my cares on Him. Again, this is a process, so do not put pressure on yourself. Every relationship takes time to develop; it's no different with Yah.

Before you move on to the next chapter, I want you to try to practice Shalach meditation. It will not only still your soul in troubled times but give you access to the peace Yah promised—any day, at any time. I recommend that you practice it after each chapter as you process your emotions and release them.

Remember, do not worry about how long it takes you or whether you're "doing it right." Just go for it and see what happens. Then, write down the three emotions that are dominant in your soul afterward. We will revisit them in the next chapter, and I will teach you how to evaluate and release the toxic ones. But for now, shout a battle cry with me: "Milchamah!" It's time to cross into the Enemy's territory and gain control of your soul.

FOUR

COURAGEOUS TRANSPARENCY

If you don't put a mask on, you won't
have to worry about it coming off.
—*Paul Singleton*

D uring an open discussion at a conference, former first
lady Michelle Obama stressed the importance for men to
communicate with and support one another. "Y'all should get
you some friends. . . . Y'all need to go talk to each other about
your stuff, because there's so much of it! Talk about why y'all
are the way you are."[1]

I agree, but unfortunately, we have been taught and conditioned to believe misleading mantras such as "real men don't
cry" or "what doesn't kill you will only make you stronger." As
a result, we suppress our emotions to keep from looking weak.
Unlike women, responsible men, especially African American
men of the Most High, do not hang out enough with their
friends. We can't even fathom planning an excursion out of

state just for fun! Many of us are so responsible that we have forgotten what fun feels like—always focusing on what needs to be done instead of what we need to do for ourselves to keep our minds healthy and emotions stable.

Men lack "safe spaces" in which we can feel free from condemnation and release what's weighing us down. But every time I've been present when men gather in a "judgment-free zone" and are encouraged to share their burdens, I've seen how one man taking a step out and expressing the heaviness of his heart can cause a domino effect. With the ice broken, the men talk for hours, and previously clogged tear ducts open up to allow tears to flow naturally, freely. But sadly, until we see the power in being transparent, we will continue to miss opportunities like this to heal from what happened and become the men we desire and deserve to be.

Evaluate Your Emotions

What three emotions did you identify when you finished chapter 3? What came up for you when doing the Shalach meditation? Keep those feelings in mind as you read this chapter.

During my Emotional Stability Training conflict resolution sessions with men, I encourage them to be vulnerable and transparent during an exercise I call "Digging for Gold." In it, I give men a "mental shovel" to dig past their surface emotions and discover the real reason for why they feel the way they do.

I urge them to choose their words carefully when expressing their feelings toward one another. Instead of saying, "You pissed me off!" I encourage them to say, "Your words hurt me, brother." It's like pulling teeth from a shark, but when men allow themselves to be vulnerable, they find deep healing from both the current offense and past ones. When we can articulate the root feeling behind an emotion, we not only respond better in conflict but also reconcile with people much faster.

Noted professor and psychologist Robert Plutchik developed the Wheel of Emotions in the 1980s. According to Christopher Pappas, "At the time, Plutchik wanted to provide a visual representation of the psychoevolutionary theory. However, since its inception, the wheel has been used by writers, therapists, and educators alike to understand the delicate balance of human emotions."[2] But in the CATTA and personally, I chose to use psychotherapist Gloria Willcox's more expansive version called the Feeling Wheel. Please google the "The Feeling Wheel" and save the image to your cell phone or computer so that you will have access to it as you go through this book.

> **When men allow themselves to be vulnerable, they find deep healing from both the current offense and past ones.**

To use the Feeling Wheel, first look at the six words in the inner circle and determine which best describes how you feel. Then, take a moment to consider which words from the second tier resonate with your current emotion. Last, take as much time as you need to look at the outer tier and decide which emotion is actually the strongest. That's likely the one you need to express.

We use this tool in the Cave to help our boys recognize

their root emotions and feel them fully so they can uproot the toxic ones and release them. For example, anger is never the root emotion for an outburst but the result of a feeling much deeper—often frustration or fear.

During the early years of the CATTA, I met Mike (not his real name), an eighth-grade student who was in danger of not graduating middle school. Mike had averaged four detentions and one suspension per month, he smoked two blunts (marijuana inside cigar paper) per week, and his grade point average was a dismal 0.8. On the exterior, all seemed well. He was funny and brilliant. But internally he was hurting, and he could only process his pain through apathy, drug use, and outbursts of anger.

One day after he had been in a fight on his way to school, I led Mike through a simple version of Shalach in which I taught him how to breathe and cast off negative emotions but keep the positive ones. I then showed him the Feeling Wheel and asked him to point out an emotion in the center of the wheel that best expressed how he felt in that moment. He chose *mad*. I then asked Mike to pick a feeling in the second tier of emotions. He contemplated for about ten seconds, then selected *angry*.

I asked Mike to reflect on those emotions for three minutes. I had noticed that Mike's father never picked him up from school, nor was his name on the CATTA's intake application. So, I asked, "How often do you talk to your father?"

Mike looked at me and replied, "Not enough."

"How does that make you feel?" I asked.

Mike said, "It hurts."

I had him look at the Feeling Wheel one last time to select an emotion in the third tier of the wheel. He sighed and said,

"Jealous . . . I want to be cooler with my dad, and it hurts some-times when I see other boys with their dads."

This was a major turning point for Mike. After his epiphany that day, I trained him twice a week for the remainder of the school year. In twenty-four weeks, Mike did not get suspended or put into detention, he stopped smoking blunts, and he improved his grade point average from 0.8 to 2.6. He even graduated on time! This is what we hope for in our training with boys, and it shows the incredible power behind deep emotional work. External struggles almost always come back to that internal battle. In my sixteen years of working with boys, I've seen that high-risk behavior is a direct result of emotional suppression. And it's the same when boys become men.

Unfortunately, most men are not good verbal processors, so we are often misunderstood or impassively dismissed. A verbal processor is a person who can vocalize their thoughts and emotions—effectively communicating why they feel the way they do. Our concerns are often heard as complaining, just as a dog's bark is annoying when no one sees trouble. Both warnings are rarely heeded before "the thief" breaks in and steals, kills, and destroys everything, even the dog (John 10:10). The Feeling Wheel is an excellent tool because it not only provides a way for us to visualize our emotions but also gives us a deeper understanding of what could be at the root of each initial feeling. If we are willing to be courageously transparent, this knowledge will give us the information needed to respond instead of always reacting when someone or something triggers an intense emotion.

—————— ≋ ——————

Being transparent—speaking openly and honestly about our emotions—is counterintuitive for most men. As children, we openly express any emotion—until we learn it isn't safe to be transparent or authentic. This happens in every boy's life, regardless of the home or neighborhood he grew up in. You may have had the most wonderful parents in the world, or you may have grown up in a single-parent home or had an abusive parent. Regardless of your home life, neighborhood, or school, you learned to survive by keeping your feelings to yourself. This happened to *all of us*.

You see, children are keen observers but poor interpreters. Whether you remember it or not, as a boy you would see or hear certain things, then you would attempt to understand what they meant. Like what it meant when a coach berated his player. Or when a father hugged his son after he struck out at bat. Interpretation is a normal part of the human survival instinct. The human brain is designed to keep you alive, and it does so in part by interpreting events and then making up "rules" to follow. Rules such as, "Don't touch a hot stove," "Don't cry in front of anyone," or "Girls aren't to be trusted." These rules are meant to shield you from physical harm, emotional pain, and social rejection. In instances of potential physical harm, or the threat of lethal violence, that's a good thing, but it's not so useful in relationships.

I'll never forget the first time I chose to be transparent with a girl back in sixth grade who said she was starting to like me.

One afternoon when we were talking on the phone, I mustered up the courage to say, "Tiffany, I really like you too. I want you to be my girlfriend." Back then, three-way calls were common, but I didn't know she had one of our mutual friends on the other line. Tiffany giggled, then said, "Jason, I was just playing with you. I don't really like you!"

I heard more laughter and realized someone else had been listening in. I literally dropped to my knees in the hallway of my mother's house. I was floored that I had been played, and I felt so embarrassed. In that moment, I vowed I would never trust another girl again.

As I got into junior high, I kept my vow. I would get into a relationship with a girl, then break up with her to get into a relationship with my best friend's ex-girlfriend. I can't even count the number of times we swapped girlfriends back then. I had successfully programmed my heart to avoid feeling love for a girl.

In the hip-hop culture, our music gradually became misogynistic, and as a popular deejay, I boldly carried my vow into adulthood. By the time I met Nicole, I couldn't even hold her hand. Nicole and I went to see a movie on our first date. Although I really liked her and wanted to make the first move, I refused to drop my guard. So, I sat with my arms crossed with Nicole's pretty face in my peripheral view. Then suddenly, I felt something brush against my shoulder; it was Nicole's arm attempting to reach around my broad shoulders. We both chuckled as I finally wrapped my arm around her. I'd been holding myself back in an attempt to be strong and to protect myself from the lie I had internalized about relationships, while what I'd wanted deep down was sitting right there waiting for me to get past my past. I know countless men who have been victorious in some way, such as in their careers, entrepreneurship, or pastoring. However, the heavy toll it took to "win" negated any sense of achievement or profit when their lives crumbled around them in divorce, alcoholism, extramarital affairs, drug abuse, or death. When we allow our emotions to master us, a Pyrrhic victory is imminent. I unknowingly used to think Pyrrhic victories were kingdom victories. But if our relationships and families are destroyed in the process, that's victory for the Enemy.

Interestingly, the exclusively male conviction of "man up" in the form of a command has been proven useless in motivating men. This phrase subtly implies that a man is already at a deficit, and the last thing a discouraged man needs is another challenge. Please don't get me wrong; I think it's good that we encourage one another to rise up when we are emotionally low. But since so many of us have been conditioned to suppress our struggles, this attempt to man up and push through what we're going through only causes more mental anguish. So, instead of manning up, we need to *open up*.

As the saying goes, the quality of your life is equal to the quality of your relationships. If you can't open up and be honest with someone about your thoughts, emotions, ideas, and opinions, you don't have real relationships. Real, heart-to-heart connection requires vulnerability, which requires courage. Yes, we are advised to guard our hearts with all vigilance, for they are the wellspring of life (Prov. 4:23), but when we go from guarding our hearts to hiding them, we stop living. And it's only when we open up our hearts that our lives begin to flourish.

Studies show that "suppressing your emotions can and does affect your body and your mind."[3] In 2013 researchers from the Harvard School of Public Health and the University of Rochester found that people who bottled up their emotions increased their chance of premature death from all causes by more than 30 percent, with their risk of dying from cancer increasing by 70 percent.[4]

Do not harden your heart to the people in your life. Instead, learn to speak the truth in love (Eph. 4:15). The four Rs from chapter 3—reflect, release, reset, and rest—can help you open up to speaking and hearing truth.

- **Reflect:** Recognize what you're feeling and breathe as you shalach every emotion that could hinder you from effectively communicating. Use the Feeling Wheel when you need help identifying the deeper emotion. For example, you might be feeling *anxious* about your new position at work, but the deeper issue is that you actually think you're *inadequate* to perform the essential duties of the job. Allow yourself to process your emotions, and you may discover the root cause of you feeling inadequate was a team member's *disparaging* comment about you in a meeting. Continue to breathe and process what you're feeling before you act—this will decrease your chances of having any regrets later.

- **Release:** If you're able to talk to the person who triggered your negative emotions, instead of yelling, "You pissed me off!" assert, "Your words in the meeting offended me, and I feel like you don't trust me. I don't try to make mistakes." This is where it takes true courage, pushing through the fear of what might happen in order to get the result you deeply desire. If you can't confront the person who offended you, talk to a friend or a counselor first. Being open and honest about your feelings can help to diffuse the negative ones and have a calming effect on your soul.

- **Reset:** Look back on how you handled the situation. Did you speak the truth in love, or did you react irrationally to your emotions? Remember, just because there's something to be said doesn't mean you should always say it. When we take responsibility for our own words and actions, we'll find ways to communicate even better next time.

- **Rest:** Sometimes being vulnerable is exhausting—mentally, physically, and emotionally. Allow yourself some time to rest, even if you only have fifteen minutes to close your eyes. Research shows that taking a power nap reduces stress and anxiety while making us more patient and alert.[5]

Please understand this is not a surefire formula for handling every conflict or offense. If you want consistently positive results, you must unlearn the toxic behavior you've been taught. Recognize the unhealthy thoughts you tend to have consistently. Notice what your own made-up rules are. Then, realize that you created those parameters—and you can trade them in for healthier ones. You can be transformed by the renewing of *your* mind so that *your* thoughts, words, and actions will be according to Yah's will and not the desires of your soul (Rom. 12:2). When you do, your responses will be effective and life-giving instead of destructive.

Courageous transparency is a strength that empowers you to openly express your emotions without fear of being admonished or condemned. Remember, it's okay for men to be gentle and strong at the same time—comprehensive manhood is the goal. When you learn how to express your emotions in a healthy way, you can become a source of healing instead of an instrument of pain.

Love Without Limits

When our hearts are repeatedly broken and desires go unmet, we begin to believe that the man in the mirror is unlovable, and the hurt from feeling unwanted hinders us from loving ourselves and others. As a result, many men are lonely today, not because they have to be but because they fear being vulnerable. I recently discussed this with a good friend of mine who is single, and he joked, "Brother, the superman cape can never come off!" Unfortunately, this same cape many of us proudly wear is now stran-

> **When you learn how to express your emotions in a healthy way, you can become a source of healing instead of an instrument of pain.**

gling the life out of us. Although my friend and many other good men desire to get married and have children, his comment further exposes why misconstrued masculinity will hinder them from experiencing the life of their dreams.

Another good brother told me he wasn't going to get married until he had his "ducks in a row." You know: his career, finances, house, and so on.

"When was the last time you saw ducks walking in a row?" I asked. We both laughed for a moment and pondered his rationale. Later that year, he proposed to the love of his life, and now they are building their kingdom together.

Please don't swerve on what I'm saying; it's honorable to have everything in order before you get married. However, it's unwise to allow what you don't have to stop you from attaining what you can. My wife and I got it together, *together*.

And if your insecurities are causing you to struggle with the woman in your life making more money than you do, I encourage you to let that go. When Nicole brought more money into our home than I could, it didn't intimidate me because money never defined my worth or our relationship. She loved me for who I was, not what I could provide.

This is the power of being courageously transparent with the one you love—you are loved and accepted regardless of what you bring, and you have nothing you need to hide. This is freeing for you and also better for both of you together. A man who can trust the woman in his life with what he has, what he doesn't have, what he thinks about, or what he fears, is able to love her and himself without limits. Trust me, there's nothing more beautiful than when two become one and build a beautiful life together.

With transparency comes healing; with vulnerability comes freedom. But sadly, many good men fear that if they are transparent with the women in their lives, their vulnerability will be used against them. This is so far from the truth. I surveyed women with this question on social media, and the response was overwhelming. A good woman deeply desires to have access to the heart of the man in her life and is willing to put forth the work needed to attain it.

The "Huddle Principle"

It is liberating to finally share your fears and insecurities with the woman in your life—and I do highly encourage you to walk down that path—but, with that said, be careful not to imprison her emotionally in doing so. Sometimes it is better to walk away and pray than to say. How do you know when to employ this?

Consider the "huddle principle" before you share something heavy with a loved one. Do you remember Super Bowl LI when the New England Patriots came back from a twenty-five-point deficit to beat the Atlanta Falcons in overtime 34–28? The Falcons had completely dominated the Patriots the entire first half. The Patriots' star quarterback, Tom Brady, who already had four Super Bowl rings and was considered the greatest quarterback of all time, was clearly frustrated on the sidelines. The hits and relentless pressure from Atlanta's defense took a toll on Brady's accuracy and decision-making, resulting in a pick-six (an interception that led to a touchdown) that gave the Falcons a commanding 21–3 lead going into halftime. Looking demoralized, the Patriots trudged into the locker room on the brink of losing the biggest game in sports.

Midway through the third quarter, the Falcons scored another touchdown, increasing their lead to 28–3. Tom Brady had to respond with the right leadership, or his team would have no chance of winning. What if Brady had approached the team huddle and said, "Listen up, it doesn't look like we're going to win this one, fellas. I'm sore as hell, and mentally I have nothing left—and no team in Super Bowl history has come back from a deficit this great!"

Can you relate? How often in life do we feel the pressure of the world relentlessly beating on us, so much so that we make detrimental decisions for ourselves and/or our families? How often do we head home feeling disheartened at the end of a workday? How are we supposed to maintain the attitude of a leader when we've received a layoff notice and we're two months behind on the mortgage?

Without question, as the team captain, Brady's words would have negatively impacted his teammates' performance, just as our pronouncements affect our families' chances of winning in life. But, instead of surrendering to the negative emotions any of us would have felt in that moment, Tom Brady rallied his team to score an unprecedented thirty-one unanswered points to win Super Bowl LI.

Vulnerability is powerful, but channeling that power so it will always be used for good requires responsibility. Please do not make the same mistakes I made. There were certain things I knew I shouldn't share because they would knock the wind out of Nicole. But due to my emotional instability, I would unload heavy issues on her that negatively affected her mental well-being and physical health. I can't stress enough the importance of expressing our emotions, but we must always be sensitive to those on the receiving end as well. Trust me, you do not want to wear down your teammates (your family), because if you do, the war within will become more difficult to win. Take the temperature of the room. Did your wife have a stressful day? Is she down or discouraged? If so, it may be best to wait until another time when your transparency and vulnerability will be better received.

You are fighting very well, warrior, but before you advance

in this war, find someone you trust with whom you can start sharing your cares. Ideally, this person should be a friend, someone you love enough to patiently listen to their concerns as well. This will not only develop your verbal processing skills but also teach you the importance of reciprocity in brotherhood. You're not the only one with problems. So, be slow to speak when it's your turn to listen (James 1:19).

Finally, there may be times when you are not able to reach your confidant or counselor. And you do not have the mental capacity to wage the war within. In these circumstances it is best to cast those cares only on the Most High. However, if your thoughts become suicidal, please do not hesitate to call the National Suicide Prevention Lifeline (800-273-8255) or visit the closest ER. Courageous transparency, with the right person at the right time, will prove to always be your best battle plan for waging and winning the war within.

Don't move! I see the enemy emotion "fear of change" stealthily approaching. It's time to shout a battle cry and yell, "Milchamah!" You've come too far to turn back now. You must fight the good fight with all vigilance!

FIVE

ABORT YOUR SHADOW MISSION

In transition, God does not lead you out of
certain seasons because they're bad, He leads
you out of certain seasons because they're over.
—J. KONRAD HÖLÉ, *WALKING THROUGH*
THE VALLEY OF TRANSITION

From the time I was fifteen through my young adult years, I desired to be a platinum hip-hop music producer, and I would allow nothing to stop me—not even wisdom. I was on a shadow mission.

For years, I ran from Yah's calling on my life and placed myself in many dangerous situations so street investors (drug dealers) could hear my music and invest money in my production company. I relentlessly stayed on this "shadow mission" until 1997 when I surrendered my life to the Most High. But even then, I still allowed the desires of my soul to keep me from walking by His Spirit.

Instead of aborting my obsession, I changed my mission from becoming a platinum secular producer who won Grammys to a Christian producer who won Stellar Awards. I continued to commit thousands of hours to developing my craft, but this time with the appearance of doing it for Christ. I was a driven man deceived by his soul.

> If we continue to leave the disappointments from our pasts unresolved, we will struggle with living fully into our potential in the present.

I made the pursuit of my passion the top priority above providing an abundant life for my family. My ceramic tile company, which provided me the freedom to travel as a producer, was very successful. I was one of the best tile setters in Detroit. However, I subconsciously allowed my company to stay small so it could never take precedence over my music aspirations. As a result, my family lived paycheck to paycheck, and though all of our needs were met, we were not financially set.

A shadow mission is an unaccomplished goal or unfulfilled desire that we continue to pursue, even when it is detrimental and hinders us from walking in the Most High's *present* will for our lives. Motivational speakers might convince you to "chase your dream until you catch it!" But the problem with this is that, too often, what they're really saying is to chase your shadow mission. That sounds inspiring, but it is a very dangerous teaching that subconsciously feeds the deceptive desires of our souls. The shadow mission is a dream that always feels unfinished, incomplete, and impossible to accomplish.

If we continue to leave the disappointments from our pasts unresolved, we will struggle with living fully into our potential in the present. And the truth is, what we may consider unfinished endeavors are actually completed tasks to the Most High. That may seem counterintuitive, but stick with me here, and I'll show you how this is true.

As a start, here are three characteristics of a shadow mission to help you begin to identify if you might be in the middle of one—and to understand why it can be difficult to abort.

- **Characteristic #1:** A shadow mission usually coincides with our deep desires, dreams, talents, and gifts. It is more about our soulish desires than Yah's will being done. This spiritual struggle between our way (the desires of the soul) and His will (resolutely walking by the Spirit) eventually births resentment and drags us farther away from His purpose. I can't imagine how much further along the CATTA would be today if I had shut down my music studio three years prior to producing my last album project. But I needed to waste more time and financial resources before I would accept the truth that being a music producer *at this stage in my life* was my shadow mission. For decades, I assumed that I couldn't live life without music, but I wouldn't trade where I am today to go back.

- **Characteristic #2:** A shadow mission is not totally against Yah's will for our lives. For instance, His will may be for you to get married, but not to the one you're still spending valuable time with. That relationship may have been simply to teach you who *not* to marry. So the hard part is knowing when something is generally in Yah's will for you but also knowing when the opportunity in front of you is not specifically the right one. One way this becomes clear is when you see that what you are pursuing is coming at the expense of your loved ones. A shadow mission is like the crafty voice of Satan that tempted Eve in the garden. Eve allowed her desire to taint Yah's truth in order to get what she wanted.

- **Characteristic #3:** A shadow mission not only reminds us of our past success but also makes us deeply desire to return to the time when our souls truly enjoyed living. It tends to pull us backward in life rather than launch us forward. King Solomon wisely advised us never to ask, "Why were the former [old] days better than these?" (Eccl. 7:10 NKJV).

Yahushua said that anyone who puts a hand to the plow and looks back is not fit for the kingdom of God (Luke 9:62). A plow is a farming tool that was created to be used in a forward motion, so the only way you can see what has been completed is by purposefully turning to look behind you. That sight can either inspire you to keep going or tempt you to stop due to what appears to be a lack of progress.

It is written that we should not dwell on past accomplishments or goals but instead press toward what is ahead (Phil. 3:13). Think of it like driving a car backward with only the rearview mirror to guide you. That's right, it's difficult to get very far.

———— ≈ ————

Contrary to popular opinion, life is not about decisions; it's about responsibility. If you're a responsible person, the responsibility should dictate what needs to be done. So, when chasing my dream of being a producer became a financial nightmare for my family, I woke up and got a good job to provide for them. When I grasped this principle, decisions became easier and my life changed—I was finally able to abort my shadow mission.

In 2005, I turned my record label into a nonprofit that today has reached more than fifteen thousand youth and families. What makes this transition a beautiful story is that Nicole is our executive director—the perfect partner for Yah's mission for *our* lives.

If you're wondering whether you are on a shadow mission, you probably are. When you are walking in Yah's will for each season in your life, you'll know it. But if you're struggling to feel sure, you can also ask yourself some key questions, like "Why am I not content?" and "Am I pretending to be something I'm not?" There will always be a level of pretense or inauthenticity present if you're in a shadow mission.

From Martial Arts to a Martial Heart

Show me someone living in a shadow mission, and I'll show you someone with an emotional wound. I know this well because I've had to abort not just one but two significant shadow missions.

I started my martial arts journey in 1982, and yet I have never attained a black belt in any of the arts I've studied. As a twelve-year-old boy in a ninja suit, I used to practice alone without a teacher. I eventually joined a school and moved through the belt ranks. Still, the elusive black belt was a mission I never quite accomplished, and it became a singular focus for me as the years wore on, even after I'd started the CATTA.

One time, when I was preparing to test for my black belt in *Aikibujutsu*, I asked my friend Paul to come to a class and critique my throws. Paul is a champion black belt in the art of judo and a great teacher. After the class, he asked, "Jason, why are you here? You don't need their approval, and you have more students than this entire school." He continued, "I made the mistake of seeking trophies, but you will have more testimonies."

I knew he was right. But I couldn't seem to help myself in terms of this shadow pursuit. I wanted that black belt, maybe even needed it. Why was that? What I didn't realize was, I had never truly been seeking the black belt or more skills, but affirmation from a father figure.

Thirty-nine years after I first began my martial arts journey, I heard Yah speak to my heart, "You were like My David, but you wouldn't allow Me to teach you." As we know, David tended his father's flock and was often alone. He testified that God trained his hands for battle (Ps. 144:1). The difference between me and David was that I resisted Yah's training and instruction. Sometimes our tunnel-visioned desire for earthly affirmation can cause us to miss receiving it from the only One who knows our deepest thoughts and can actually answer all our doubts. And sometimes Yah speaks through other people.

One summer, I decided to devote the long hours necessary

to refine my punching and kicking mechanics. My instructor at the time, Professor Jawwaad Muhammad, gave me a key to the dojo because of my commitment. Every morning for two months, I would execute one hundred reps of four different kicks and one hundred reps of four different punches—on both sides.

Within a couple of weeks, I could see major improvement in my form and striking power, but I still felt like I was missing something. One morning as I was going through my regimen, Professor Jawwaad walked in, took a seat, and watched silently as I trained.

I still had energy after my last set of kicks, but my emotions caused me to collapse on the floor. "Why won't you help me?" I asked Jawwaad. With an empathetic look on his face, he responded, "If I told you that you have everything you need, you wouldn't believe me." Professor Jawwaad never really liked the belt ranking system. He actually tried to eradicate it from his school because he believed it distracted the student from the real purpose of training—sort of like how the shadow mission thwarts Yah's true purpose for our lives.

A few years prior, I'd had a similar experience with our chief instructor, Kajana Cetshwayo. For years I would ask Chief to work with me one-on-one. I always thought I needed his help in order to accomplish the Most High's purpose for the CATTA, so one day in the parking lot of the dojo, I pleaded one last time for Chief to teach me.

He replied with a smile, "When the student is ready, the teacher will appear." This is a classic saying in martial arts. Although I understood the principle behind it, I felt hurt and dismissed by his short response to my plea. Almost instinctually

I thought to myself, *If the teacher isn't there, he will never know when the student is ready.* And I walked away feeling dejected. In fairness to Chief, he had more than seventy students at the time and had trained quality black belts to help him teach; I was just one of many men who desired his personal instruction and affirmation.

But then that one summer morning years later, Professor Jawwaad gave a second response that not only contrasted what Chief had said but was also prophetic: "When the teacher is ready, the students will appear."

Prior to that day, I only had twenty students, but today as I write this, the CATTA has over four hundred and fifty boys on our waiting list and a national demand to scale the academy across the United States. I've been a guest on several national talk shows, and I was even acknowledged at the White House for our Emotional Stability Training. None of this would have happened if I had stayed on my shadow mission of attaining a black belt. I would have been more dedicated to a martial art than to saving boys. More importantly, the credit for my success would have gone to a sensei or coach instead of the Most High. My shadow mission deceived me into thinking that I needed to be a master of a martial art to do what I am doing today. But all the Most High needed was a man with a martial heart—a man who fights to rule every emotion that hinders Yah's love from freely flowing from his heart!

My true calling was always far greater than martial arts accomplishments, but my longing for fatherly affirmation compelled me to seek a sensei instead of the Most High. For too long, I subconsciously tried to fill the void my dad had left in my heart. But when I allowed Yah to father me, my father wound (trauma inflicted by our fathers) finally healed, and I walked out of my shadow mission and into His will. Now I resolutely walk in my purpose and no longer allow my quest for affirmation to determine my destination. I will expound more on what this healing process looks like in chapter 9.

Defeating Giants

We all fear change to some extent. Instead of moving on, we allow our emotions to deceive us into staying in a "season" that has already fulfilled its purpose in heaven (ministry, friendships, work, etc.). As with my music-producing aspirations, remaining in a season that has passed will cause frustration, hurt, and disappointment. However, when we allow the truth to sober our souls, we will stop wearing sandals in the winter and a wool coat in the summer.

If I had stayed on my shadow mission, millions of people would not have been blessed and inspired by the CATTA's viral videos; NBC's hit TV show *This Is Us* never would have used the father and son push-up ceremony I created; and the iconic actor Laurence Fishburne wouldn't have wanted to film a documentary on my life. I also wouldn't have written *Cry Like a Man*; our nonprofit, the Yunion, would not have been able to purchase and renovate our fifteen-thousand-square-foot building; and I wouldn't be writing this book right now. This is just the start of what Yah has done since I yielded to His will, and the list goes on and on.

Some of the best decisions I've made are the ones my friends and mentors did not agree with. This does not mean they were deliberately trying to give me bad advice; it's just that they are not always right. It's important to listen for Yah's still small voice as you process your choices.

For instance, when David was about to fight Goliath, his "mentor," King Saul, advised David to wear the king's battle armor—a bronze helmet and a coat of mail. Out of respect, David put everything on and strapped a sword over the armor. After taking just a couple of steps, David knew if he wore Saul's armor he would die at the hands of the mighty Philistine champion, Goliath. "I cannot go with these, for I have not tested them," David said to Saul (1 Sam. 17:39 ESV). Then David took off the heavy battle gear.

Remember, everyone has a soul but not everyone has their soul under control. Many mentors, friends, family members, and even elders will try to complete their shadow missions through you. This is why it's imperative that you have a relationship with Yah. You need to be clear on what He is saying to you. People, especially those who love you, may sincerely want to help you fulfill Yah's purpose for your life but end up pressuring you to do it *their* way. As a loving father, I completely understand this rationale. All good parents want to protect their children, so we naturally question anything that makes us fear for their well-being. But it's never a good thing to veer away from the way the Most High is leading you, even if His way doesn't make sense to people watching from the sidelines.

Saul offered David his own armor in order to protect him. But Saul was unaware that David's sensei was the Most High and David had years of training in Yah's "dojo" that prepared him for this fight with Goliath. "You are not able to go against this Philistine to fight with him," Saul exclaimed. "For you are but a youth while he has been a warrior from his youth" (1 Sam. 17:33 ESV). But David boldly informed Saul, "The LORD who delivered me from the paw of the lion and from the paw of the bear, He will deliver me from the hand of this Philistine" (1 Sam. 17:37).

David chose to do what he knew, in the way the Most High had already been teaching him. He picked up five smooth stones from a stream and put them into his shepherd's bag and ran to fight Goliath. David did not allow what he had become good at (tending his father's flock) to become his shadow mission, nor did he allow anyone to live theirs through him. With one stone, slung from one sling, one boy defeated a giant who terrified many—and the rest is history.

Confusion exists when we do not know why we exist. So, I pray this chapter has given you the wisdom to identify your shadow mission and empowered you with the faith needed to step out of it and into the light of Yah's *present* will for your life. But I forewarn you, as soon as you try to advance, your inner enemy, "fear of change," will attempt to bombard your brain with toxic thoughts in hopes of shaking your soul. When this happens, shalach every emotion that will hinder you from boldly moving forward into the next chapter of this book and your life.

Now shout a battle cry and yell, "Milchamah!" because this next battle will require you to face and purge what makes us retreat when we should stand firm.

SIX

PURGING PASSIVITY

For God has not given us a spirit of fear and
timidity, but of power, love, and self-discipline.
—2 TIMOTHY 1:7 NLT

Recently, one of our CATTA recruits shared how he
defended himself against an assault at school. Josiah is a
beautiful boy with an infectious personality, but not everyone
in his school viewed him like that. Due to his small stature,
cute face, and kind heart, Josiah was a prime candidate for
being bullied. Sadly, he was a victim for years. Inside, Josiah
had a fiery spirit, but like I did before I broke free from emotional incarceration, he assumed it was evil to be assertive.
This all changed when he ceased allowing his fear of being
perceived as a bad guy to stop him from doing the right thing:
defending himself.

The school bell rang, and Josiah prepared for his next
class. Abruptly, a boy twice his size forcefully grabbed him

from behind. Within seconds, Josiah responded to his attack with a judo technique called *O-goshi* (major hip throw), and the bully landed on the floor before he could even react. That day, everyone in our academy, including the parents, celebrated Josiah's victory over abuse and passivity. But my heart felt doubly blessed when he took pride in the fact that he had been able to thwart the attack without severely injuring the bully. Just before the bully's body hit the ground, Josiah pulled up so the boy's head would not hit the floor. Josiah was on his way to becoming a comprehensive man—courageous and compassionate, strong but also sensitive, a man who freely lives from his heart and not his fears.

King Solomon wrote, "The wicked flee when no one is pursuing, but the righteous are *bold as a lion*" (Prov. 28:1, emphasis added). Godly anger, or righteous indignation, is a very powerful emotion. It can empower us to run fearlessly toward righting a wrong or even ignite movements against injustice; but if not channeled correctly, it will bring harm to its possessor and others (Eph. 4:26). This is why in the CATTA we teach that aggression is untamed power, but assertiveness is a calculated action that keeps you in an advantageous position. The latter is our goal! And it is what Josiah displayed that day.

Unfortunately, many good men do not know how to channel their righteous indignation into a calculated action, so they "play it safe." But being a coward not only makes living this life miserable, it is also spiritually detrimental. Yahushua warned in Revelation 21:8 that the cowardly will not enter the kingdom of God.

I'm not suggesting that you put up a front and refuse to acknowledge your fears, as I've clearly established that transparency is a power that liberates us. However, we were also created to be bold when necessary. A man who has to walk on eggshells to keep peace will eventually become so skilled at it, that he makes no sound in life. Too many men have mastered the innocence of a dove but stay novices when it comes to being shrewd as snakes—Yahushua said to be both (Matt. 10:16).

> **Aggression is untamed power, but assertiveness is a calculated action that keeps you in an advantageous position.**

This is one of the main reasons why I believe so many men live unfulfilled lives. We allow the safety that our souls desire to restrain Yah's radical Spirit within us. We stay lukewarm when we should be hot (fiery against evil) or cold (refreshing to those who are oppressed). So, do not be misled by false humility. A Christian coward is worse than a gangster who snitches (Prov. 28:1).

If you want to keep peace, you must be willing to fight introspectively to purge the emotions that make passivity your home.

———≈———

Passivity is often a manifestation of a skewed view of humility. For the sake of appearing humble, I used to allow people to make sly remarks in my presence without checking them. But when I got home, I would unfairly transfer the indignation *they* should have received onto those who didn't deserve it—my family. I was the very definition of a passive-aggressive male, and being a man of the Most High seemed to make it worse because passivity was preached from pulpits more often than assertiveness.

Sometimes referred to as "quiet strength," humility keeps us from expecting more than we deserve and reminds us to be thankful for everything we receive. Humility prevents us from being prideful and helps us lean into Yah's grace when we are weak.

However, humility is not having such a low view of yourself that you allow others to dominate you. As meekness is not weakness, passivity is not humility. Passivity is often at the root of people pleasing, which causes us to behave inauthentically for something we will never attain. The unhappiest people I've ever met are those who try to make everyone happy—which is an impossible task.

———≈———

Since 1997 when I surrendered my life to Christ, I've noticed that passivity appears to plague more men of the Most High than others, so let's address the elephant in the room. Pusillanimous teachings in the church have encouraged many strong men to willingly castrate their masculine attributes for the sake of looking nonthreatening. As a result, we subconsciously do the same to Yahushua, the *Lion* of Judah. Although there are many teachings of Yahushua that have been misconstrued, Matthew 5:39 is by far the pinnacle: "Do not resist an evil person; but whoever *slaps* you on your right cheek, turn the other to him also."

Let's look at this. Why did Yahushua say the right cheek? During biblical times, most people were right-handed, and the left hand was used for unclean tasks. So, in order to slap someone's right cheek, a person would use the backside of their right hand. A backhanded slap was a way of scolding somebody who was out of line in those days. The intention was not to injure but to humiliate, to put someone in his or her place.

In the three examples Yahushua gave in the following verses (Matt. 5:40–42), He never alluded to a slap on the cheek as causing serious physical harm. So, theologically, turning the other cheek is unmistakably a response to a reprimand or an insult. It is not cowering from a fistfight or physical threat.

In a broader context, Yahushua was a threat to the Roman Empire, and Rome was not passive in its actions to eradicate potential uprisings. This is why many biblical scholars believe Yahushua told His disciples to sell their garments and buy swords (Luke 22:36).

Another passage that gets taken out of context is when Yahushua told Peter that those who live by the sword will die by the sword (Matt. 26:52), which ends up being used as a justification for being passive. Yahushua was saying that those who live for violence will die by it—not that a man who protects himself or his family will die because he did so.

If Yahushua had been preaching passivity, He would have been called a hypocrite when He made a whip out of cords, assertively turned over the money changers' tables, and chased them out of the temple (John 2:13–16). The very fact that not one of those men tried to fight Yahushua speaks volumes about His fiery spirit!

And yet, instead of producing valiant warriors of Yah who can articulate their faith and boldly demonstrate it, the church has unintentionally produced men who are sensitive but not strong, compassionate but not courageous. We now have a generation of untested intellectuals who can academically articulate their faith, but when faced with real confrontation, they choose passivity like Saul's army instead of godly assertiveness like David. No wonder evil runs unchecked in today's society! Instead of whining for Christ to come back, which, by the way, we are told not to do (Amos 5:18–19), we need to fight with all vigilance to expose every work of evil in our lives and this world (Eph. 5:11). This is why, when a recruit in the CATTA loses the fortitude it takes to push through a difficult test, I remind him that faith is all theory until it's been tested—and so is love.

We must learn to exude both sides of Yahushua: the *lamb* when compassion is needed and the *lion* when injustice is upon us! I love the way my friend Paul Coughlin said it in his book *No More Christian Nice Guy*: "We need to see and emulate all of Jesus, gentle and rugged and all points in between."[1] When Christ walked the earth, He was no doubt a comprehensive man, and when we allow ourselves to be the same, we'll become better men ready to help those in need.

Faith is all theory until it's been tested.

Stop Shrinking Back

In 2013, I attended a life-changing men's retreat with twenty-one broken men in dire need of healing. One of the first exercises the staff had us do was to break into teams of five. They asked us all to stand, then directed each group to choose a leader without speaking words. Those who felt they were not the leader were to take a seat, and the one man who remained standing was to be the team's leader. After a minute of staring into one another's eyes, two of the five men on my team sat down. I felt that I could lead the team, but I didn't feel confident enough to remain standing after that. As soon as I moved to sit down, though, the remaining two men sat simultaneously before I could bend my knees. At that moment Yahushua asked me, "How long will you run from the position I have called you to?"

After each team leader was selected, we were sent out on a challenge course in the forest. The team that was the first to complete the tasks and return to the firepit were the winners. Throughout the early stages of the test I kept saying to myself, "We are losing," and my soul kept telling me, *Someone else should have led this team!* When we finally made it back to the firepit, I didn't see any of the other teams. "Man, we must be in last place," I said aloud. And my soul echoed, *I told you someone else should have led this team. You failed your dad so many times, and you failed these men too.*

Then one of the counselors grabbed his walkie-talkie and announced, "We have the winner!"

At that moment, I dropped to one knee and began to cry without composure—giving Yah the glory for helping me overcome the lies I believed about myself. Afterward, the camp counselors asked the team members what they liked the most about their leader. One of my teammates, a retired special forces paratrooper, said:

- "Jason listened to our suggestions."
- "He delegated to our strengths."

- "He led us with confidence even when he didn't believe."
- "He asked our guide all the right questions."

These are the testimonies Yah has for all of us, but we must be willing to put on His full armor and shout the battle cry while running toward the war that wages within. When we stop succumbing to passivity and yielding to self-doubt, we will be able to boldly express the good we've been hiding from the world.

Be True to Yourself

To celebrate our twentieth wedding anniversary, Nicole and I decided to go to Hawaii. I'm not a fan of water activities, especially in the ocean, but I let Nicole talk me into taking a tour of some of the most beautiful sea caves in the Na Pali region that also included snorkeling. It took about twenty-five minutes to get to the best destination for snorkeling. Unfortunately, the choppy waves made Nicole seasick, and she spent the remaining four hours lying nauseated on the floor of the boat.

As everyone else on the tour jumped into the water with excitement, I asked the tour guide, "How do you keep the sharks away?"

He laughed and said, "We can't."

I smiled as I took a seat to comfort Nicole.

With a baffled look, he asked, "You're not going to jump in?"

"I don't need any extra adventure. I was born and raised in Detroit."

Almost instantly he came back with the classic, "Don't be scared, man!"

I replied, "Although fear is relative, I am not scared in this moment. I choose to be comfortable rather than to conform. I'm a black man who has experienced a lot of trauma—I don't need adventure on my vacation. I desire serenity and relaxation."

Intrigued by my response and resolute demeanor, he asked, "What do you mean?"

"How many years of experience do you have navigating these waters?" I asked.

He proudly responded, "Almost my entire life! My father started this business when I was a child—he took me on every excursion to learn the waters and the business. Now I'm the tour guide, while he and my mother manage the company."

"That's awesome! Can I ask you another question?"

"Sure!" he responded.

"How often do you travel outside of Hawaii?"

He answered, "Maybe twice in my life."

"What if you took a trip to Detroit and I was your tour guide? During the tour, your bladder becomes painfully full and you ask me to stop the vehicle so you can relieve yourself. As you get ready to exit, you observe your surroundings and ask, 'Is this area safe?' Then I respond, 'Sure! There are gangs in this area, but don't be scared; there hasn't been a shooting here in months.'"

After the longest ten seconds of silence, he smirked and said, "I get your point."

People will always try to persuade you to do what *they* are comfortable with. Stop allowing people to bind you to things you do not want to do—plundering your desires and, more importantly, derailing your purpose. Trust your own instincts. Stop going along to get along; if you keep doing what you do not feel comfortable with, you will harbor anger and resentment toward yourself and others. Passivity prohibits you from telling others what you think and need. Remember, no one is a mind reader, so speak up.

Be Assertive

Nicole and I enjoy good food, so we dine out often; but it takes more than a well-prepared meal for us to enjoy the experience. If the waiter or waitress is not in the mood for serving, the night could be ruined. For years I would stay passively silent when we received bad service. Then during the ride home, I'd be angry, sometimes yelling because I had settled for subpar service instead of speaking up.

Now, instead of allowing someone else to ruin my day, I take command of the moment. To my surprise one evening, I discovered that my speaking up was what the waitress needed.

"Excuse me. You appear to be in a bad mood, but my wife and I desire to have a great dining experience. So, could you please ask your manager to switch you with someone else?" The waitress froze in shock, clearly unaware that whatever was going on in her personal life was visibly evident in her behavior.

"Sir, I am so sorry!" she exclaimed. "I'm upset because I had to leave my four-year-old daughter at home with her grandmother. I work so many hours trying to provide for her that we rarely have time to bond."

"I completely understand," I responded with empathy. "I used to work ten to twelve hours a day, six days a week for

Coca-Cola, and I could only see my daughter for a couple of hours a day."

With tears in her eyes, she said, "Thank you for sharing that, and I promise, if you give me another chance, I will do my best to make this a great experience for you and your wife." And she kept her word!

The next time someone serving you appears to have a poor attitude, respectfully speak up and be assertive. You may be surprised at how your voice could make their day, resulting in a memorable experience and another victory over passivity.

It's Okay to Be Dominant

I've trained in several martial arts since 1991, and my favorite by far is Brazilian jiu-jitsu (BJJ). Initially, I was excited to learn how to defend myself effectively when taken to the ground in a fight, but soon I was even more intrigued at how BJJ aligned with so many key life and biblical principles.

How often will a man be down in life and need to get up before his circumstance, vices, or unresolved trauma beats him down again? According to King Solomon, "a righteous man falls seven times, and rises again" (Prov. 24:16).

So, my desire for learning BJJ was not to learn how to *stay* on the ground when in a fight, but how to arise physically when taken down by an attack or mentally when weighed down by a personal trial. Therefore, I tell the CATTA recruits to act as if the ground is four hundred degrees hot; the longer you stay down in a street fight, the more vulnerable you are to more threats from the attacker's friends. And the longer you stay downtrodden in life, the more susceptible you are to depression or suicidal thoughts.

I started private lessons with my friend Tyrone Gooden, one of the most experienced BJJ black belts in Detroit. But since his school was far from my office, he suggested that I enroll in a BJJ school in my area to get experience grappling against multiple people. The 313 Brazilian Jiu-Jitsu was the last school I would join before I completely dedicated my time to creating and finishing the CATTA's curriculum. I became good friends with one of the owners/coaches and Marcelo Garcia black belt, Zander Heinen.

Unlike the other martial arts I've studied where you can execute your techniques without someone actually trying to stop you, BJJ commands its practitioners to fight one another with real resistance. So, passivity has no place in it, there is never a "day off," and you work hard in every class. I was sold! Physically, I would know for sure if my techniques worked, and internally, I would wage war to keep my soul under control. Yah used BJJ to purge my passivity completely.

One day Yah prompted me to subdue everyone I rolled (sparred) with. This is a rare accomplishment in any good BJJ school, especially for a three-stripe white belt. Talk about an inner war! Since I'm a teacher at heart, I caught myself showing one of the men I rolled with what he was doing wrong and then teaching him how to beat me. How crazy is that? Believe it or not, I still managed to tap him out before the buzzer sounded, ending the round.

As I took a moment to gather myself before meeting my next opponent, I heard Yah say, "Jason, as long as you stay passive when I need you to be powerful, you will never fulfill My will." I then remembered how Jacob relentlessly wrestled an angel of Yah until he was blessed (Gen. 32:24–32). I said to myself, "Passivity is not of Yah," and tapped out everyone I rolled with. It felt good to finally let the lion out of the cage of passivity—it was a blessing worth fighting for. Drenched in sweat, I

> **Passivity not only prohibits us from living from our hearts but also keeps us from being the leaders we are meant to be, responding with the right action at the right moment.**

praised Yah for coaching me that day and thanked Zander for always being a source of encouragement. I was a different man.

I no longer feel guilty when I am bigger, stronger, and more skillful than my opponent—that's his problem, not mine.

—————≈—————

Passivity not only prohibits us from living from our hearts but also keeps us from being the leaders we are meant to be, responding with the right action at the right moment. To illustrate this, I love the scene from *Avengers: Age of Ultron* in which the ground is crumbling around Black Widow and Bruce Banner (the Hulk), threatening their lives.

Bruce grabs Black Widow by the arm and says, "We gotta move!"

Black Widow turns and asks, "You're not going to turn green?"

"I've got a compelling reason not to lose my cool," Bruce replies passively.

Black Widow smiles and says, "I adore you," and passion- ately kisses him just before forcefully pushing Bruce into a deep crevasse.

"But I need the other guy," she states as he falls.

Black Widow then stares into the chasm, anticipating the inner beast in Bruce to arise. The Hulk suddenly appears from the abyss, strong and dominant, and carries her to safe ground.[2]

This world is in dire need of good men who aren't afraid to dominate when a situation requires them to do so. Days before King David died, he told his beloved son Solomon to "show yourself a man" because he felt that Solomon lacked the courage and boldness needed to be the next king of Israel (1 Kings 2:2). Also, when the Spirit of the Most High fell on His prophets and kings, they did not become passive but were filled with righteous indignation (Judg. 14:14–15; 1 Sam. 11:6). They were dominant!

As long as you're passive, you will never summon up the courage it takes to yell a convincing battle cry before your enemy. You must first believe before you can achieve. Take a moment to breathe deep and imagine claiming victory over passivity in your life. Allow yourself to feel powerful in this moment. You're not tired of living; you're tired of *not* living. Now yell, "Milchamah!" because it's time for you to make another advance in this war. There's no turning back now.

Before you turn the page to the next chapter, write down three areas in your life in which passivity prevents you from being adamant about what you want, need, or deserve. (For example, maybe you don't speak up when a coworker steals credit for your work or you don't take that first step toward pursuing the woman of your dreams.)

Then practice Shalach and reflect and release until you are able to get to the root emotion of—or reason for—your passivity. Look at the Feeling Wheel if you need help digging deep. Confide in a comrade—the person you've chosen to be courageously transparent with. Articulate your thoughts; convey your concerns. This could be the difference between victory and defeat on the internal battlefield.

Warrior, it has been said that communication wins wars,[3] so in the next chapter I will teach you how to *express* what you've been taught to *suppress*.

SEVEN

COMBAT COMMUNICATION

A hot-tempered man stirs up strife, but he
who is slow to anger quiets contention.
—*Proverbs 15:18*

As much as I enjoy training in Brazilian jiu-jitsu, my time training under Chief Instructor Kajana Cetshwayo is what conditioned my mind for physical and mental combat. Chief was a no-nonsense, fiery, Vietnam War veteran with a tested reputation in the streets of Detroit. Although Chief was a skilled fighter, his masterful way of teaching principles intrigued me the most. One of them—combat communication—I still practice daily in my marriage and in other relationships as needed.

Combat communication is the "language" that comes from the exchange of information during a fight between two combatants. The fighter who pays attention and mentally downloads the other's strengths, weaknesses, and tendencies will be equipped with the data needed to respond to his opponent's attack and put himself in the best position for victory.

For instance, if your opponent tends to flinch every time you fake a punch or kick, this data informs you that he is likely anxious, respects your power, and/or lacks confidence in his own defense. This information allows you to then upload techniques and strategies that could set your opponent up for a knockout or submission. In the same way, when we rule the emotions of our souls and are able to maintain self-control, we will see each situation in front of us clearly, untainted by our fears or desired outcomes. Then we can mentally download the data from the other person's actions to help us resolve the conflict at hand, instead of always being on the defense.

This is what I do when I'm engaged in an argument with my wife. No, Nicole and I have never fought physically, but we both have been guilty of verbally hitting each other where it hurts. I can't count the times I only listened to Nicole in order to respond, instead of intently listening to what her *heart* was actually saying. Nicole and I used to have so many emotional triggers that, as soon as one of us was offended by our actions or words, we would pull out the guns of our past and start shooting each other from our unhealed wounds. Our counselor called us "trigger happy," which the dictionary defines as "recklessly advocating action that can result in war"—or in this case, marital discord.[1]

But now, when Nicole throws verbal jabs, I introspectively bob and weave to avoid the impact of her words so I can respond in a patient and understanding way that allows us to communicate in love. Yes, it takes two people to make a marriage successful—no one will be able to hold with two hands that which requires four to carry. However, I've discovered that when a husband becomes a comprehensive man and communicates his true feelings with composure, his wife is able to drop her guard and do the same—knowing that each other's intent is not to harm but to express what offended them.

Combat communication not only teaches you how to respond advantageously but also gives you the ability to process several possible courses of action before you commit to one. It will take discipline to intently listen. And by listen, I don't mean simply hearing the words spoken—I mean discerning the intent behind the words. At the same time, you'll have to observe a person's body language. And then, when you still your soul, you will be able to ponder every outcome that could happen as well as every action you could take.

If the situation is tense, know that you cannot depend on your mind because its main goal is to protect you, not necessarily help you make the best decision for the moment.[2] So, you must clear your mind and still your emotions, keep your composure, and respond resolutely. This is what it means to be an emotionally stable fighter.

---≈---

You might not consider yourself a fighter, but every one of us encounters conflict in our lives. We all find ourselves in situations of miscommunication or misunderstanding. Combat communication can help you create the best possible outcome in any conflict, and sometimes it can help you avoid conflict altogether.

For example, I was with my son, Jason, one day at the building we had recently purchased for the Yunion. I had just locked up and was enjoying my time with him so much that I was oblivious to my surroundings. Suddenly, I heard a voice behind me say, "Someone is trying to kill me!" My instincts fired up immediately because I had never met this young man before, and since I am licensed to carry a concealed firearm, I drew my gun. "Who's trying to kill you?" I asked the young man.

"They're coming around the corner," he said to someone on his cell. Then I noticed a gray Chevy Suburban driving toward the building.

"Wait a minute!" I exclaimed. "So, you're gonna bring them to me around my son?" I immediately started playing out scenarios in my mind, and I could tell something was off with his claim. He was too calm, especially with a phone to his ear.

If someone is coming to kill him, why is he standing still on the phone, and who is he talking to? I thought. Meanwhile, the SUV was coming closer, and all I could think was my beloved son's life was in danger. In the streets of Detroit, you never know when someone might start shooting. I knew I needed to get Jason back inside the building quickly, but the door lockset was old and unpredictable, and I had to insert the key just right before I could unlock it. I stilled my nerves enough to get the door open and get Jason inside while the Suburban was still driving toward us. Jason did not know the seriousness of this situation, but he knew something was wrong. Once he was safely inside, I looked at him through the small glass window in the door and said, "Son, everything will be okay. Walk to the back of the building."

Imagine looking into your son's eyes, seeing his fear, and not knowing if you will see him again. Think about the emotions you would feel, then having to abruptly still them so that you could respond and not react emotionally to a coming threat. Having done all this, I turned around and noticed that there were three men in the Suburban as they made a U-turn back toward us. With my peripheral still on the young man, I got into a modified Weaver stance (an assertive gun position) and used my truck as a barricade just in case the people in the Suburban opened fire. Then, as they slowed down in front of the building, they made another U-turn in the opposite direction. As they drove down the street, the young man started jogging in the same direction.

So, you're going to run in the direction they're driving? I thought, concluding that they were probably trying to set me up to carjack my GMC Yukon that was parked out front. I was new in the neighborhood and appeared to be an easy target until I pulled out my gun. The way things played out, the likely assumption is that the young man was on the phone with the men in the SUV and told them to abort. Thankfully, I didn't have to harm anyone that day, and I was able to still my soul and maintain self-control in order to thwart the threat. I then opened the door and firmly hugged Jason, praising Yah for His protection.

Listen, Perceive, Evaluate

I used to be a facilities manager, mentor, and security guard for a charter high school in Detroit. My boss was what some would call a type A personality. One morning, I set up the conference room for an important meeting he was having with the leadership team of the school, then left to attend to other duties.

Unfortunately, I accidentally left the conference room door unlocked, and a mischievous student snatched an opportunity to sneak in and write profanity on the tablecloth. My boss called me and requested that I return to the conference room immediately. When I arrived, I noticed the leadership behind him as he stood, holding the tablecloth with a look of disdain on his face. For approximately two minutes, he berated me like a child for allowing someone to enter and deface school property.

I wanted to "dog check" him in front of his superiors for talking disrespectfully to me, but "keeping it real" sometimes goes wrong, and I had made a mistake. I not only needed to keep my job to provide for my family but also wanted to continue mentoring students at the school. So, instead of reacting from my feelings, I chose to counter his tirade with a respectful response. "I'm sorry, sir. This will never happen again." I smiled respectfully at his superiors as I exited.

After their meeting adjourned, my boss came looking for me. He yelled my name from across the campus as he rushed toward me. "Jason, I was an [expletive]. I never should have talked to you that way. Everyone in the meeting was so upset that they reprimanded me for ten minutes straight! I am sincerely sorry."

Although my boss and I made amends that day, he still sometimes seemed to delight in making me feel inferior. One day after school, my employee failed to show up for work on time, leaving the school unsecured during the busiest hours. I was later informed by a teacher that he often left duty when I was not on site. Due to the possible liability I could have faced, I decided to cancel my security contract with the school. This upset my boss, and instead of simply giving the contract to someone else, he called for an emergency meeting and deducted additional money from my biweekly pay for managing the school's facilities. Although I was angry and wanted to argue against his actions, I remembered that "it is an honor for a man to keep aloof from strife, but every fool will be quarreling" (Prov. 20:3 ESV). Since reason had no seat at the table, and it was clear that nothing I could say would change his decision, I stilled my soul, stared into his eyes, and silently sat so I would not delay the adjourning of this meeting.

The next day, Yah honored my self-control in the form of a certified letter stating that our nonprofit, the Yunion, would receive discretionary funds for a federal grant for mentoring, for which we had previously been denied! Nicole and I yelled in disbelief but praised the Most High for responding swiftly to my defense and providing a pay raise that doubled what I was making at the school. I submitted my two weeks' notice the following week, and, although it felt good to be out from under my old boss, I felt bad for him. He was a good man inside and I learned a lot from him, but unfortunately, his words would often cut more than heal.

Again, in any situation, combat communication allows you to listen, perceive, evaluate possible outcomes, then choose your words and actions advantageously. And before you dismiss it as a "nice idea" or as something that only men trained in martial arts can do, I'd like to tell you a story.

Combat Calamity

On Wednesday, September 18, 2013, two men in Ionia, Michigan, died needlessly as a result of road rage. Nobody knows exactly what happened, except that the two men pulled over in a parking lot and started arguing with each other before gunshots were heard. Both men had concealed carry licenses, and as the argument escalated, they drew their guns and shot each other. One man was forty-three, the other fifty-six. Both were pronounced dead at the scene.[3]

I want you to take a moment now and put yourself in that heart-wrenching scenario. Imagine thinking about your actions while you're lying in your own blood. What would you have done differently? Whose faces would you see? How would they be affected by your death? What memories would flash through your mind as you shed tears of regret and took your last breath? Would protecting your ego really have been worth it?

Listen up, men. Emotional instability can get you killed. If it doesn't kill you, it will destroy your relationships, your health, and your future. It will hurt your family, your friends, and your community. On the other hand, emotional stability and combat communication can not only save your life but help you live and love without limitations and without fear of detrimental consequences. These tools unlock your power to wisely wage and win the war within.

I, for one, had to learn some of this the hard way.

Nicole and I were talking in our kitchen one day when I announced with passion, "I need to start spending more time with little Jason."

Nicole paused and looked up at me. "I wish you desired to spend time with me like you do with him."

In that moment, what I "heard" was that I wasn't doing enough for her. I felt accused, judged, and condemned in less than ten seconds. I didn't hear that she was longing to be with the man she loves. My emotions raced out of control, and, in a rage, I hit the refrigerator so hard that I dented the stainless steel. "Be quiet! Don't say anything else!" I yelled.

Nicole's countenance fell, and she slowly sat down at the kitchen table, obviously crushed at my irrational reaction. Her demeanor got my attention, and something shifted inside me. I had always protected her, yet she clearly didn't feel safe in that moment, even though she knew I would never hurt her physically. I realized that I have the force in my voice and in my appearance to crush someone's spirit.

That incident almost cost me my marriage.

In my uncontrolled anger, I couldn't hear Nicole's heart. I only heard my own emotions. And because of that, I literally saw my wife break down in front of me. I vowed it would never happen again. This is why I practice combat communication every day, in my marriage and in other situations. "Death and life are in the power of the tongue" (Prov. 18:21). Therefore, bless instead of curse, and speak life instead of allowing your words to bring forth death in your relationship or purpose. This is one of the essences of combat communication.

———— ≈ ————

Instead of evading my internal battles, I choose to face them so Nicole and I can experience the peace we do today. Sadly, to avoid conflict, countless couples sweep their marital issues under the rug for temporal peace instead of seeking counseling. This is why I believe you'll see people married for thirty-plus years get divorced after their children leave the house.

Psychologists attribute conflict avoidance and "going along

to get along" as two of the top reasons for the influx of divorces.[4] Nicole and I have heavy hearts for all the couples who love each other but are finding it difficult to communicate their love during unprecedented times. Decades of marital issues that had been "swept under the rug," like infidelity, mismanagement of money, and poor communication, resurfaced due to the COVID-19 lockdown.

If you happen to be under that kind of stress in your marriage or romantic relationship, here are some combat communication keys you can use:

1. **Do not listen in order to respond to her words.** Listen to her heart instead. Try to discern what she is really trying to express.

2. **Believe her intention.** During a moment of marital discord, I tell myself that Nicole loves me and doesn't mean to harm me. This allows me to respond from my heart instead of my fears.

3. **Check your ego.** Just because you have something to say doesn't mean it should be said. Do you really need to be right? Can you take responsibility for your words and actions? Do you need to apologize?

4. **Give each other space.** Take a walk, take a breath, practice Shalach—maintain that meditative state while moving. Take inventory of your emotions—*reflect, release,* and *reset*—before you speak. Cool off, pray for discernment, then revisit the conversation.

5. **Reconcile immediately.** Do not allow emotional wounds to fester into sinful actions (Eph. 4:26). Still your soul so you can rule your emotions and reconcile with your wife

or significant other. Do not give the devil an opportunity to destroy what you've longed for (Eph. 4:27).

Life with loved ones can be so fulfilling when you're willing to work through conflict of any kind. Combat communication helps us convey love more than compromise.

Nicole and I celebrated our twenty-second anniversary in the midst of the COVID-19 pandemic. Even though cases were reportedly resurging in our area, Nicole still wanted to eat at a fine-dining restaurant, but I wasn't comfortable with that.

I asked, "Is there something else we can do?"

With her hands on her hips, she retorted, "I don't want to do anything then!"

I paused for a moment to still my soul so I wouldn't react emotionally. I understood that Nicole, like millions of others, was just trying to get back to normalcy. Practicing Shalach daily allows me to have a large capacity for offenses and keeps me emotionally stable during unsteady times. I waited for a better time to express that I felt her response wasn't loving or considerate of my thoughts regarding COVID-19. When we did have that conversation, she agreed, expressed her reasoning for her response, and we reconciled.

> **Combat communication helps us convey love more than compromise.**

Since I didn't suppress my emotions regarding Nicole's response, I was able to think clearly and come up with another option for dinner. For me, in marriage, a compromise isn't doing something you do not want to do but finding a common ground that doesn't compromise your convictions, especially those given to you by Yah. So, rather than not spending quality time with my wife on our anniversary, I chose to go to the restaurant with Nicole, planning to keep my mask on and not eat.

After we were seated, the manager and staff not only made us feel safe, but seated us outside where tables were set ten feet apart. We had an amazing time! If I had allowed my emotions to rule me in that heated moment, or not communicated them with love and conviction at the right moment, we would have stayed home and missed out on a wonderful evening.

———— ≈ ————

As men and emotional beings, we must understand that we are not the only ones involved in any communication—it's a two-way street, and sometimes we have to cross over to the other side to assess what's going on.

A man can endure a slap in the face, but a wounded heart causes him to guard his love forever. During this journey to freedom from emotional incarceration, your wife or the woman in your life may misinterpret your concerns as complaining, or she may impassively dismiss your emotions.

When this happens, it is important not to respond by going to another woman to share your cares unless she is a trusted family member, professional counselor, or therapist. You may ask, "But what about my friend Lisa? She always listens to me." I strongly caution against this, unless your wife can join these conversations. If the goal is reconciliation, this should not be an issue for you or Lisa. However, if you feel uncomfortable with your wife being present, you're probably sipping on poison. "The lips of an immoral woman are as sweet as honey, and her mouth is smoother than oil. But in the end she is as bitter as poison" (Prov. 5:3–4 NLT). So, instead of flirting with temptation, practice combat communication with the ones you love and watch how it transforms your heart and relationships.

Communicate Love

I used to parent with a hard hand, and I never considered the cause and effect of my children's actions or lack thereof. In my mind, they were wrong if they didn't meet my expectations. Eventually, after years of biblical counseling and prayer, I realized this was not Yah's way for a father to raise his children. The Bible teaches, "Fathers, do not provoke your children to anger by the way you treat them. Rather, bring them up with the discipline and instruction that comes from the Lord" (Eph. 6:4 NLT). As I mentioned in chapter 1, discipline without love is ineffectual. No child wants nor deserves a "dictatorship dad" but a loving father who conveys the discipline and instruction of his heavenly Father with grace.

Because I felt I had to perform for my own father's love, I became a parent who demanded perfection instead of helping my children learn how to process the emotions that caused them to be disobedient or make mistakes. One morning during breakfast, I noticed my son anxiously studying to retake a spelling test on which he'd previously scored low. I despise multitasking, but I encouraged him for his effort and told him to focus on finishing his meal. As I was putting on my coat, I noticed Jason intently studying again as we were getting ready to leave. The old dad would have yelled and rebuked his disobedience, but I realized that my son was performing for my love and affirmation. Using combat communication, I walked up to Jason, embraced him, and said, "Look into my eyes, son. You do not have to perform for my affirmation. If you failed every test, I would love you even more." A tear rolled down his smooth cheek, and I kissed him on his forehead and prayed.

That afternoon when I picked him up from school, he ran toward me with a huge smile, saying, "Guess what, Dad! I got a 100 percent on my spelling test!" I lifted him up in the air and proudly celebrated his success throughout the halls of his elementary school.

When we live from what we longed for instead of what we lacked as children, we can unreservedly communicate the love we deeply desire to express to our own kids. I no longer desire to be a perfectionist or demand perfection from my children. Instead, I am an "excellentist," someone who strives for, and encourages, excellence but leaves perfection to Yah.

Communicate Forgiveness

By now, you've seen how effective combat communication can be. However, it's even more powerful when paired with the principle of forgiveness.

When people forgive, we tend to exude higher levels of patience and self-regulatory skills.[5] I can attest to this because when I forgave my dad for verbally abusing me as a child, I was freed to father from my heart, not my wounds. One evening I had to work late and could not eat dinner with Nicole and

Jason. As soon as my last meeting adjourned, I washed my hands and eagerly started preparing my plate. As I went to grab a glass, I noticed my son standing over the stove eating a chicken wing—*my* chicken wing!

This upset me because it was not only an inconsiderate thing to do, but disrespectful. I work hard to provide a good life for my family, and my six-foot-tall twelve-year-old doesn't pay one bill! I would have done him a disservice if I didn't discipline him. However, in the process of sternly rebuking his behavior, my heart was forgiving him—and minutes afterward he and I were laughing again.

When we combine forgiveness and combat communication, our anger in a moment will no longer ruin the day. Holding on to offenses emotionally incarcerates us, but forgiveness is a key that liberates. Allow the latter to free you from those who did wrong in your life so that you can get on with yours.

Applying Combat Communication Daily

Perhaps you've heard the common saying, "Your ego will get you killed." While that's absolutely true, as evidenced by the two Michigan road ragers, it's also true that our egos can destroy our marriages, our health, our finances, our careers, and other significant relationships.

Just because God is good all the time doesn't mean life is good all the

> **Holding on to offenses emotionally incarcerates us, but forgiveness is a key that liberates.**

time. Problems and conflict will happen, and with them, emotions will arise.

Here's an easy way to remember combat communication: listen, look, and learn before you leap.

- **Listen**—to what someone is saying; not only their words, but their heart.
- **Look**—at the whole picture: body language, facial expression, and other cues.
- **Learn**—to discern the possible scenarios and outcomes.
- **Leap**—to take the wisest action that comes to mind for the best outcome.

One of my favorite scenes in *Avengers: Infinity War* is when Doctor Strange goes forward in time to view the future for all the possible outcomes of the upcoming fight with supervillain Thanos. Out of 14,000,605 combat options, Doctor Strange reports that there is only one winning scenario.[6] The scene itself is a fascinating picture of how fast the human brain works. This is good to remember when we're facing potential conflict.

When my boss berated me in front of his colleagues, there were many ways I could have reacted to his offense, but I chose the best *one* in that moment to keep me and my family in the best position. Likewise, my deep desire is for you to be able to process several outcomes to a decision within seconds before you have to make it. Whether you're faced with physical conflict, your child's disobedience, or an argument with the woman in your life, you must wage and win the war inside instead of responding in pride.

"Do not be overcome by evil, but overcome evil with good" (Rom. 12:21). I pray that you learn to thrive in life as an emotionally stable fighter, one who combats through communication before acting.

You are now learning how to fight the good fight—wisely waging war within so that you no longer have to live without the freedom to feel. But stay alert, warrior, for "your adversary, the devil, prowls around like a roaring lion, seeking someone to devour" (1 Peter 5:8), and he has just deployed the weapon that has destroyed the greatest of men: sexual temptation. So yell, "Milchamah!" because his actions have communicated it's time to battle again!

EIGHT

SEXUAL SELF-CONTROL

He who reigns within himself, and rules
passions, desires, and fears, is more a king.
—*John Milton, Paradise Regained*

My father was a six-foot-tall, dark, and handsome man. As a kid, I admired his physical strength, but he was not the best role model to show me how a man should treat a woman. I often wondered, *How many women does it take to please one man?* He was a popular barber in Detroit and also quite popular with the ladies. As a kid making extra money sweeping up hair, I would hear men in the shop brag about their sexual conquests and boldly express misogynistic viewpoints. My father would chime in with his own glory stories—and he practiced what he preached.

After Mom and Dad divorced because of his cheating, I would rarely see my father with the same woman for more than a month. His promiscuous ways subconsciously taught me that women were sex objects to be used and manipulated by men, not favor from the Most High to help us accomplish His will (Prov. 18:22). In the beginning, when Yah saw it wasn't good for man to be alone, He created Eve to be his "help" (Gen. 2:18 KJV). The Hebrew translation for the word *help* in this verse is *ēzer* (ay'-zer),[1] which means to surround, protect, or succor; assistance and support in times of hardship and distress.[2] This is why *ēzer* is the same word we use when referring to the Most High as our "help and shield" (Ps. 115:9 NLT). Sadly, much due to our insecurities, many of us would rather have women play the role of a slave than a source of strength who helps us push through our inadequacies.

Accompanying my dad's whorish behavior was his dogmatic demeanor. My father had a bad temper and would stay ready to verbally engage with anyone who countered his opinion, or physically fight at the slightest offense.

Although my father was no longer living with us, some of his mail would occasionally come to our house. One day, as my mom and I were walking out the door going to school, she anxiously reached into her purse and pulled out a .38-caliber revolver handgun. "Jason," she said, her voice quivering. "I opened your father's mail, and he's very angry right now. He may come over this morning to try to hurt me. I wanted to show you this so you will not be surprised if I shoot your father." She didn't, but she left me worried and traumatized for the rest of the day. Just think, I was on my way to school with all of this on my mind. How could I focus? Students are often misdiagnosed with ADHD due to unresolved trauma.[3] And sadly, until we as adults get professional help to resolve ours, intergenerational trauma and its negative consequences will continue.

By the time I turned twelve, I was no longer focused on my grades—just the girls. My hormones were racing, and without a mature man of the Most High in my life, I quickly became addicted to X-rated magazines. My first encounter with one was at my father's house, and masturbation came without a lesson. Our propensity to sin from birth is deep (Ps. 51:5).

I was so eager to feed my addiction that I would steal X-rated magazines from stores with zero conviction or fear of getting arrested. The feeling of having the most beautiful women literally at my fingertips and under my "control" was a temptation I couldn't resist. This evil desire pulled me into the dark world of porn. We didn't have the internet, so it was challenging to get access to pornography, but there was always an owner of a video store who would hook me and my friends up for the right price.

Eventually, my lust had to expand beyond imagination, turning into an unhealthy desire for the real thing. When I reached the eighth grade, my friends and I had no self-control. We would grope girls aggressively in the back of the classroom as if it were a game. I'm utterly disgusted to even admit this today, but it's imperative that I be transparent and expose the evil that was in me (Eph. 5:11) so that you will not hide if you do the same. I am living proof that you can be delivered from sexual sin.

The girls, many of whom were our friends, would try to laugh it off, but in hindsight, I realize they were offended. Occasionally, one would yell in anger, garnering the teacher's attention, but we would plead with them not to tell—and they wouldn't. This sickens me as I type this because countless women are silenced by fear, displaced guilt, or powerful men when sexually assaulted. Reflecting on my actions in eighth grade makes me wonder if that fear was instilled in them at a young age.

By the time I was a senior in high school, I'd had sex with many young women, and prom was the opportunity to sexually engage with a new one. Angela (not her real name) was attractive and attended a different high school. We met through a mutual friend and, lucky for me, Angela hadn't accepted any invitations to prom. My kindhearted nature won her over, and she said yes when I asked if I could take her to her school's prom—but first I had to meet her father. He and I got along well, and with my mental fingers crossed, I vowed to not touch his beloved daughter on prom night.

As I was leaving their home, Angela's father said, "Oh, by the way, I know your dad. Please tell him I said hello." *Why did he wait until I was leaving to mention this?* I wondered.

I drove straight to my father's barbershop to ask him about this. When I mentioned Angela's father's name to my dad, he chuckled with a devilish grin. "Yeah, I know him. We used to be good friends."

"What happened?" I asked, baffled at his expression. "I'm supposed to take his daughter to prom."

My dad told me he had visited Angela's parents one afternoon. After a few drinks and laughs, Angela's father needed to make a quick run and left my father alone with his wife. My father took offense to the fact that his friend had the audacity to leave him alone with a beautiful woman.

"He must have thought I was a punk! But I had my way with his wife that day," he bragged to me. I didn't know how to process what I was feeling. My father not only committed adultery but did so with his friend's wife, then boasted about it. And although I was promiscuous, and championed the lifestyle, something finally convicted me about the way men viewed sex and women. My father was wrong—I was wrong.

Prom night arrived, but I chose to leave the condoms at home. I now saw Angela through a different lens. Her innocence was to be respected, not taken advantage of. I picked Angela up from her house and, like a gentleman, escorted her to my car and opened the door for her to take a seat. We had a great time that night, and because my mind wasn't perverted with sexual thoughts, I was able to see that Angela was meant to be someone's wife someday. But I wasn't ready for that, so out of respect for her and her father's wishes, I gradually and gracefully ended the relationship when she left for college.

We've Been Deceived

When there's a lack of good male role models, boys will copy what's being modeled for them, whether by the men in their lives or by their culture. Having grown up in what's considered the golden era of hip-hop (1986–1997), I was exposed to misogynistic mentoring, which unfortunately affected my mind as a young man. Popular axioms like "bros before hoes" and "money over b's," propagated by many misguided hip-hop music artists, subconsciously programmed us to objectify women and deactivate any emotion that encouraged a genuine love for them. Though I started seeing things differently on prom night, this mentality still lingered and had a negative impact on the early years of my marriage, making my thoughts toxic and hindering me from expressing heartfelt love for my beloved Nicole.

If we remain slaves to our emotions, we will continue to destroy not only the stability of our homes and communities but also our own bodies. Could you imagine being in a boxing match where every time you hit your opponent you felt the blow you delivered? Warriors, this is what happens spiritually when we practice sexual immorality. We sin against our own bodies (1 Cor. 6:18). Yeah, it feels good to "hit" what we're aiming for, but when the emotional smoke settles, the consequences of our actions cause us to flee like cowards from the debris of broken hearts and homes. Yet to this day, countless men celebrate the lothario lifestyle—obsessively seducing and deceiving women to affirm their own manhood. Yah did not create women to be used but to be loved!

Yah Creates, Satan Perverts

A pastor friend once preached that "God gave Adam a *responsibility* (the garden) but gave Eve a *relationship* (Adam)." Do you grasp the depth of what he was saying? At the time, Adam did not know that it was *not* good to be alone, but the Most High did. So, He created Eve from Adam, not to work with him in the garden but so that Adam could experience the reciprocal blessings of a relationship. But when a man holds allegiance to the masculine mandate, he cannot access the gamut of God-given emotions needed to cultivate the connection that allows him and his wife to truly become one.

I'm often asked to be a panelist for discussions centered

around men's health and behavior. A few years ago, I accepted an invitation to a large men's conference in the South. The topic was centered around saving fatherless boys, but the discussion never touched the root cause of their fatherlessness—until I spoke up. "It's troubling my soul that we've spent almost an hour talking about saving our sons, but we haven't mentioned loving our wives." I continued, "We keep putting the cart before the horse. We are so focused on saving Cain and Abel that we do not discuss how to reconcile Adam and Eve! It's a heart issue. We are supposed to love our wives as our own bodies. We are doing a terrible job because we don't love ourselves." As soon as I said that, men across the room said, "Wow" in somber unison. The *truth* will set us free, not what we *want* truth to be.

The key to finding real love is to first search in the mirror. With the help of many counselors, I learned how to love myself, and as a result, I was finally able to reciprocate the love Nicole gave me. Our marriage was no longer a mirage but a beautiful vision of Yah. No longer just a state contract to have sex but a covenant with the Most High.

Have you ever wondered why, during sex with a woman or your wife, you might think of another woman you had sex with in the past? There is a spiritual reason for this. Every time you have sex with a woman, you become one with her in body. Literally, two become one (1 Cor. 6:16). How ironic is it that in your quest to get a "piece" of that woman, you spiritually got a piece of that woman? Sex was not meant to be a superficial act, and we are not merely animals with sexual instincts.

No, human sex between a man and a woman is meant for two to become one in a sacred spiritual connection called marriage. There's a reason why Solomon, considered the wisest king ever to live, advised his sons, "Share your love *only* with your *wife*. Why spill the water [ejaculate the sperm] of your springs in the streets, having sex with just anyone?" (Prov. 5:15–16 NLT, emphasis added). But even Solomon had his struggles with sexual self-control. Eventually he began practicing polygamy, especially with women from different nations, which was forbidden by the Most High. His sinful desires led to his downfall and the kingdom being torn away from his son (1 Kings 11:1–13). I've seen the same sin play out in men's lives and their sons' futures, so I chose not to follow in my father's footsteps.

In 1994 I decided to stay with a friend in Atlanta to pursue my music career. On one occasion, his roommate invited strippers over for an exclusive gentlemen's party with unrestrained sexual activity. I declined to join and stayed in my room to make music. As I was finishing up a song, one of the strippers knocked on my door and asked if I wanted her to dance for me. I was not interested. My disinterest perplexed her because she was very attractive and well known in the Atlanta area.

Without permission to stay, she sat on my bed and stared at the wall. Within minutes, she started sharing her heart with me and how her initial plan was to dance until she could make enough money to start her own business. Unfortunately, money lures many away from the light, and she was misguided, lost in the dark arts. I gave her a few ideas on how to create an exit strategy from the strip club. She wanted to stay in touch, but I loved Nicole and I knew what scriptures teach regarding avoiding the very appearance of sin. She respected my conviction, and because of our conversation, she decided to leave the party early.

I share this story because, regardless of the choices *they* make, women were not created to be treated as sex objects. We are supposed to view them as our future wives—not less than, but equal partners (1 Peter 3:7). So, the next time you encounter a misguided woman, I pray you will see a wounded soul instead of someone you can manipulate and control.

Training Up Our Sons

I am often approached by good-hearted millennial men, both black and white, who desire to make a positive impact in the African American community. After allowing them five minutes to share their passion, I stare at their left hand and ask, "So, where's your ring?" Perplexed, they look down at their hand and laugh. Without condemning them, I say, "Son, it's encouraging to see your desire to restore our communities, but healthy families are the foundation for any thriving community. You build the community from your family first." Within minutes, these young men open up and share their reservations regarding marriage. Later in life, many of them testify it was that conversation that gave them the confidence to live from their hearts and not their fears—resulting in marrying the love of their life.

The last thing we need in the black community is more actor-vists: people who play the role of an activist, but whose lothario ways prevent the sustainable change we need.

I cannot emphasize enough: our sons will emulate our actions—so as long as we allow our own lack of sexual self-control to go unchecked, as my friends did in Atlanta, our sons will continue in becoming men who not only leave innocent women traumatized but also perpetually make detrimental life decisions. And there is a cost. There is always a cost. It is written, "A man without self-control is as defenseless as a city with *broken-down* walls" (Prov. 25:28 TLB, emphasis added). In ancient times, cities were protected and fortified when they were surrounded by stone walls. So, without self-control, a man is vulnerable to living an at-risk lifestyle, or maybe I should say *deathstyle*.

It troubles me that, to this day, promiscuity and misogyny are not the main topics discussed at every youth or men's conference. Men, how can we build what we desperately need when we as a whole are not actively confronting the lack of sexual self-control in our boys and men? Do we not recognize that the lack of sexual self-control is the root cause of STDs, fatherless children, broken homes, and disconnected communities? It's a good thing to teach a boy how to tie a tie, but it's imperative that we teach him to rule the thoughts that make him desire to have sex with every woman he sees! We've lost our way.

Instead of sacred, sex with a woman has become equivalent to putting another trophy in our mental display cases—our egos. The phrase "trophy wife" is undeniably insulting to Yah's masterful creation of the human being through which He chose to birth life in His image. The Most High created men and women to live together with a perfect love that casts out fear (1 John 4:18), not for one of us to demean the other. And our sons should be taught and *shown* the same. There's a saying that children don't do what you say, they do what you do.

And, to make it worse, when practiced immorally, sex becomes a gateway, like street drugs—you will always need another hit when the high goes away, causing you to desire more, with more frequency, intensity, and perversion. I pray you are taking this chapter seriously, because if we do not gain sexual self-control ourselves, our sons will never see us as men of the Most High. Instead, they'll see men who are in and out of their mothers' legs and lives—and they will repeat our pattern. But when sex is done Yah's way, and you can access and freely express all of your emotions, it heightens the intimacy that plays out not only in the bedroom but also in your daily interactions with your wife. A flirtatious smile, the holding of hands, arousing talk, and tender touches. Believe me, the best way to save our sons is to faithfully love their mothers and commit to family.

Christian Nestell Bovee said, "Example has more followers than reason."[4] In other words, our sons hear what we say but watch what we display.

Evading Temptation Before It Hits You

Blocking a punch in martial arts can be effective; however, you must be physically stronger than the person delivering it, in order to withstand the impact. In contrast, maneuvering on a punch not only keeps you from getting hit, but also puts you in a position to counter or control the attack. When we flee the very appearance of sin (1 Thess. 5:22), we decrease our chances of getting tapped out by temptation.

Of course, this is easier said than done, but what isn't

> **Our sons hear what we say but watch what we display.**

easier said than done? Stop making excuses when you hear good advice that's hard to apply. Instead, fight with all vigilance to preserve your integrity, marriage, family, and life.

I've mentioned the successful ceramic tile and marble company I owned. My craftsmanship and attention to detail brought me into many homes occupied by single and married women who flirted or pursued a sexual relationship with me. One time I literally had to walk away from a $25,000 kitchen remodel when one of my customers boldly insisted, "I can't have you in my house if you're not interested in being more than my tile guy!"

In another situation, a wealthy married woman walked naked across the bathroom floor to take a shower while I was still applying the grout to the tile joints. And by the way, this was not the only full bathroom in their home. There will always be opportunities to sin, but as a man of the Most High, I fight to always look beyond the desires of my soul to maintain sexual self-control.

We all have opportunities in our daily lives to practice evading temptation. For example, I love LAY'S plain potato chips. One day during my low-carb diet, I walked past an unopened bag in my kitchen. I said to myself, "A few chips won't hurt." As soon as I went to open the bag, I heard the Holy Spirit ask, "If you can't deny these LAY'S, how you gonna deny those legs?"

This is how our souls set us up. First, it's the flirting, then the calling, then secret meetups, then you know what. Warrior, as long as women live, sex isn't going extinct. Do not be anxious and rush the process. I am a witness that good guys don't finish last, they finish just in time for a woman who patiently waits. So, if you're a virgin, keep your power! If you're not a virgin, save your remaining power for your wife.

Crimes of Passion

The recent wave of sexual misconduct allegations in the national news proves that countless men have become so obsessed with power that they resort to desperate actions to acquire women they cannot have. So many of us men have become so obsessed with the "freedom" of being promiscuous that we willingly allow our physical urges to birth desperate actions in order to acquire the "love" of a woman we cannot have. As a result, like Amnon in the Old Testament, we eventually become mentally and spiritually ill. Second Samuel tells us, "Now David's son Absalom had a *beautiful* sister named Tamar. And Amnon, her half-brother, fell *desperately* in love with her. Amnon became so *obsessed* with Tamar that he became *ill*" (13:1–2 NLT, emphasis added). When our deceptive charm fails to get what we desire, we use demonstrative force that turns our sisters into victims.

Since Amnon was stronger than Tamar, he raped her. Then *suddenly* Amnon's "love" turned to hate, "and he hated her even more than he had loved her" (v. 15 NLT). He shouted for his servant and demanded, "Throw this woman out, and *lock the door* behind her" (v. 17 NLT, emphasis added). Tamar was wearing "a long, beautiful robe, as was the custom in those days for the king's virgin daughters. But now Tamar tore her robe and put ashes on her head. And then, with her face in her hands, she went away crying" (vv. 18–19 NLT).

Unfortunately, this kind of behavior didn't end in biblical times. Today, every two minutes, a woman in the United States is sexually assaulted, and one in five women will experience sexual assault or rape during her time at college. The survivors of sexual assault are three times more likely to suffer from depression, six times more likely to suffer from post-traumatic stress disorder, twenty-six times more likely to abuse drugs, and four times more likely to contemplate suicide.[5] Sexual self-control needs to be addressed vigilantly if our daughters, wives, sisters, families, and communities are to thrive.

Tamar's torn clothes represented mourning and loss. The ashes on her head were an outward sign of internal sorrow and distress. Lastly, Tamar laying her face in her hands and crying represented shame.

Does this sound familiar? It seems that we, the "leaders of the village," have subconsciously thrown our sisters out like Amnon did and locked the door behind them. And because we refuse to open the door and right our wrongs, women are shamed into silence—undervalued in a culture that coerces them to live under the oppressive conditions of inequality.

It's hypocritical for us to practice a promiscuous lifestyle and have a misogynistic mindset while living as a community, church, or political leader—or to occupy any position that requires integrity and morals. Before we can "open the door" that leads to the healing of women's hearts, we must first humble ourselves, repent for the evil we have done and allowed, and pray for forgiveness from the Most High so that our minds can be renewed. When we turn from our evil ways, then and only then will our homes and communities be healed (2 Chron. 7:14).

Desire What Is Really Important

I found it interesting that the king who wrote the famous "virtuous woman" passage did not describe her by *physical* attributes but instead said, "beauty is fleeting" (Prov. 31:30 NIV). Here was a man who could have had virtually any woman he desired, but he longed for the one woman who was "hard to find." Because his desire was aligned with why the Most High said men shouldn't be alone, this king sought something more valuable than beauty. In the book of Proverbs, King Lemuel described the virtuous woman, most likely to open our spiritual eyes so we can see how we've been deceived—and what (or who) we should desire instead.

According to Proverbs 31:10–31, here are the attributes of a virtuous woman:

- She is *hard to find* (v. 10).
- She is worth *more* than jewels (v. 10).
- Her husband *trusts* her (v. 11).
- She brings her husband *no evil* (v. 12).
- She is a *hard* but skilled worker (vv. 13–14).
- She *builds* her own resources, an investor (vv. 16 and 24).
- She is *skilled* at spinning wool (v. 19).
- She is *compassionate*, gives to the needy (v. 20).
- She *provides* necessities for her family (vv. 21–22).
- She dresses with *class* (v. 22).
- Her husband is respected *because of her* (vv. 23 and 31).
- She is an *entrepreneur* (v. 24).
- She is *mentally strong* and *dignified* (v. 25).

- She has a *wise* tongue (v. 26).
- She is wise and *responsible* (v. 27).
- She is *praised* in her home (v. 28).
- She is *above* average (v. 29).
- Her value is *not* in her beauty or charm but in her fear of Yah (v. 30).
- She bears *good* fruit (v. 31).

Warrior, our masculine attributes are from the Most High, but when we lack self-control, we misuse a power that was meant to empower us and make others feel safe. Your position as a man may make you feel important; however, it's your character that makes you invaluable. If you're searching for a Proverbs 31 woman, you won't be able to find her until you become a Proverbs 31 man—someone who truly values and welcomes all that a woman is worth.

> **If you're searching for a Proverbs 31 woman, you won't be able to find her until you become a Proverbs 31 man.**

Now yell, "Milchamah!" because the Enemy has been exposed. Attack and take rule over your emotions and hold captive every toxic thought that tries to prohibit you from unlearning what you've been deceived to believe. Remember, you are not alone in this fight. You should only wage war with wise guidance, and victory lies in the multitude of counselors (Prov. 24:6). So, during the purging process of toxic habits and trauma, diligently seek professionals in counseling and psychotherapy to undergird your efforts.

You're very close to victory, warrior, but now it's time to practice Shalach before you go into the next chapter of this war. As I said in chapter 3, *reflect* on every convicting emotion that arose during this chapter, *release* the shame so that you can implement the action needed to become a better man, then *reset* so your heart will be open to receive the affirmation you've longed for.

NINE

ACCEPTING AFFIRMATION

Never allow the mistakes you've
made, stop you from being celebrated
for the good that you've done.
—*JOHN DAVIS*

On Father's Day 2017, Nicole asked me to stay in bed until she called for me to come into the living room. Our entire family was in Traverse City, Michigan, for a weekend vacation, relaxing in a beautiful suite with an amazing view. Unbeknownst to me, my daughter, Alexis, and son, Jason, were rushing to finish decorating the suite's living room and cuing up a video they had made of themselves sharing special words of appreciation for me.

"Come on, Jay!" Nicole yelled, her excitement obvious.

When I stepped out of the bedroom, I couldn't believe my eyes. They had made the entire area look like a birthday party, complete with black balloons, gold streamers, and wrapped gifts. You'd think I would have been overwhelmed with joy, but I was the opposite. I felt so unworthy of the effort that was put into this moment. The plethora of mistakes I had made as a husband and father, coupled with the decades of rarely hearing anything encouraging from my father, always made it difficult to accept affirmation from anyone. With a huge smile on her face, Alexis embraced my arm and walked me to a chair positioned in front of the television mounted over the fireplace, then pushed play.

On the exterior, I had to look calm and appreciative because Alexis and Jason were watching me intently, but internally I could feel a war raging. My soul said, "Jason, guard your heart. No one loves this much." But Yah's Holy Spirit countered, "Jason, allow yourself to be loved. Just because you were neglected as a child and made mistakes as an adult does not mean you're not valuable."

One after another, personal messages played on the screen—from Nicole, Alexis, Jason, and a couple of boys to whom I am a surrogate father. I tried my best not to cry, but my tear ducts reached their capacity and I broke down as I allowed my soul to believe all of their words of affirmation.

The day before, I had posted a meme of two hamburgers on social media that juxtaposed the way Mother's Day is celebrated versus Father's Day. The one on the top was a delectable filet mignon burger with lobster, romaine lettuce, and special sauce on a perfectly toasted bun. The bottom burger, which represented Father's Day, was a trampled McDonald's cheeseburger in a smashed and cracked bun. Although the image was hilarious and garnered over 6,000 likes, I noticed that, in many of the 253 comments, men expressed how it hurt to feel devalued. Women compassionately shared how they desired to "do this" for their husbands or "do that" for their dads, but how the men in their lives always resisted.

Warrior, I don't know about you, but I can't tell you how many Father's Days I thwarted my family from planning anything special for me. They would ask me what I wanted or needed, and I would reply, "Nothing." It took me years to understand that, when my father did not affirm me, he subliminally taught me that I was not worthy of any form of affirmation. I eventually realized I wasn't simply going to get over this. When I finally got tired of living with a hardened heart, I did the hard work needed to soften it. I participated

When we do not love ourselves, we eventually start condemning ourselves.

in various therapies as if my life depended on them. I went to individual counselors and life coaches for personal guidance, to psychotherapy to release trauma, and to marriage counseling for my family.

Honestly, loving my wife and children was never the hard part. Loving myself was. And regrettably, when we do not love ourselves, we eventually start condemning ourselves. How many times have you cursed yourself out for making another mistake or failing at something you worked so hard to accomplish? Self-condemnation not only hinders us from loving without limits but also prevents us from receiving the affirmation many of us need to heal our emotional wounds.

As long as we blindly follow the masculine mandate, we will continue to pop open an emotional umbrella whenever family, friends, or work colleagues—especially men—shower us with affirmation.

When I was a guest on Van Lathan's podcast, *The Red Pill*, we had a powerful discussion about the African American community and what needs to be done for black men to heal from racial terror and generational trauma. As Van was closing our discussion, I thanked him wholeheartedly for not only supporting my work in the CATTA but also risking his career to shed light on injustices around the world.

I called him a hero. Almost instinctively, Van tried to deflect my words of praise. "Naw! Naw! Naw!" he interrupted me abruptly. His reaction to affirmation was a direct result of what many men, regardless of ethnicity, struggle with—loving ourselves. So, I continued speaking words of affirmation to him.

"Receive it! You are a hero; you are a soldier, and I salute you. That's the beginning of healing. Accept who you are."

With palpable sincerity in his eyes, Van reached out, shook my hand, and said, "Thank you so much."[1]

When we cannot receive love and affirmation from one another, we will never be able to attain the healing we so desperately desire. Living in a state of heartache wearies the soul and takes the life out of living. I know this pain so well, which is why I *reflect*, *release*, and *reset* daily so I can heal comprehensively and stay whole. How often do we as men, especially African American men, deflect affirmation instead of receiving it? When you see one black man encouraging another, it typically goes like this:

Brother #1: Yo, what's up, King! I'm proud of you,
bro. I love how you're handling your business.
That was a great investment. You're the man!

Brother #2: Naw, brother, you're the man! I love the
way you're handling your business!

Instead of one brother receiving the affirmation and holding it so he can grow in confidence, he quickly passes it back. Within a matter of seconds, the conversation looks like a lateral play in football.

Brother #1: No, you the man!

Brother #2: Naw, bro, you the man!

Brother #1: No, good brother, you are the man!

And on and on it goes.

It's deep how we can long for affirmation for so long that we don't even know how to *keep it* when we receive it. We toss the ball to someone else before we can get tackled.

Understandably, when society labels us deadbeats or refers to our wives as the "better half," it's difficult to believe and receive words that express good things about us. This deflective defense mechanism was developed during our formative years when we needed affirmation the most.

Imaginary Heroes

Affirmation is the foundation on which a son's confidence is built, and it's not a coincidence that, when a boy does not receive affirmation from his father or a man, he seeks it from wherever he can. He might find acceptance and camaraderie in joining a gang. Having sex with multiple women may make him feel empowered. And selling drugs may lead to death or imprisonment, but the risk makes him feel brave. A father to a son is like a map on a road trip. With a map, you can see your options, possibly avoid going the wrong way, and take the safest and most sensible route to your destination. However, without a map, you will experience frustration and misdirection, you may possibly never reach your destination.

Sadly, this was my story.

I was a twelve-year-old boy in a ninja suit in my backyard practicing alone without a teacher. Not my desire, but no one in Detroit taught ninjitsu. I didn't realize then that Yah was training me like David, so my longing for human affirmation caused me to relentlessly pursue martial arts into my thirties to find the affirmation that hadn't come my way. I was skilled but never stayed under one teacher long enough to attain a black belt in any of the arts I studied. I was a "mixed martial artist" but not by choice. I wanted to master one style and have an allegiance to one sensei. But almost every teacher I had would do something that upset me, and I would stop training under them.

Yah eventually showed me that it was my fear of being disappointed by a man that subconsciously caused me to abort training before my heart would develop an allegiance to a father figure. And believe it or not, I would blame Yah for not sending me a man to teach me how to be one. Again, this is what happens when we stay in fight-or-flight response—our hearts will stay guarded even when the Most High sends us someone to help us heal. This greatly hindered me for so many years, and it wasn't until I spoke at my stepfather's funeral that I realized I was the one blocking Yah's blessings.

In 1982, my mother married Mr. Alfred Crum and things were all good between him and me until the untamed testosterone of my teenage years, coupled with my father wound, caused me to rebel against his authority—I even pulled a shotgun on him one day. My unjust actions eventually drove him and my mother to divorce. Mr. Crum and I reconciled years later, and when he died, it was only right that I pay my respects at his funeral. When the time came to give two-minute remarks, I walked to the back of the line at the podium. Person after person testified about Mr. Crum's God-fearing character. As the last person was finishing their remarks, I got lost in reverie as I pondered the years Mr. Crum had eagerly taught me how to play sports, wash cars, and tie a tie.

It was now my turn to speak, but before I could utter a word, I became overwhelmed with tears. Then Yah spoke compassionately to me, "Jason, it was I who sent Mr. Crum to father you, but the hurt from your biological father's absence wouldn't allow you to be healed through him." By this time, I couldn't stop my tears from flowing as I shared with everyone in attendance what had just been revealed to me. After the funeral, I drove around Detroit for an hour crying tears of regret. It was a hard lesson but one I was thankful to have finally grasped.

Recently I've been meditating on the second half of Proverbs 17:6: "The glory of children is their fathers" (ESV). This verse resided in my spirit after viewing stats on fatherless kids. The word *glory* in this verse means "beauty, renown, and honor."[2] It could also be translated as "boasting." Although I would rarely see my father, I can remember as a child always boasting about how great he was compared to my friends' dads, and they likewise would do the same. Our fathers were like imaginary heroes in the neighborhood that we hoped would swoop down and love us one day. It never happened for me, but today it can happen for you and your son.

Father-Son Affirmation

Affirmation is so important for a man's development that the Most High spoke audibly twice to affirm His son, Yahushua, in front of men: "You are My beloved Son [Yahushua], in whom I am well pleased" (Mark 1:11 NKJV), and "This is my Son . . . Listen to him!" (Matt. 17:5 NIV). Due to the lack of affirmation in my life, I began to search for significance in all the wrong places. The majority of boys I've mentored over the years have lived the same way.

The Most High never desired for us to live without our earthly fathers present; that's why it is written: "[God is a] father of the fatherless. . . . [He] settles the solitary in a home" (Ps. 68:5–6 ESV).

This promise prompted me to study fatherlessness in the Bible. I quickly discovered that there were many fatherless mighty men of the Most High who overcame their "father wound." Take Joseph, for example. He could have let his fatherless circumstance (approximately thirty years without his father, Jacob) give birth to anger, self-pity, and resentment toward his brothers and his father. But instead he allowed our

Father in heaven to father him. As a result, Yah was with Joseph, showing him steadfast love and giving him favor throughout every trial. Near the end of Joseph's life, he testified before his brothers that all that was meant as evil against him, the Most High used for good (Gen. 50:20).

The emotional pain I experienced from never being able to please my father tainted the way I viewed my heavenly one. I simply did not trust Yah and became angry every time I heard someone say, "God is in control, and what the devil meant for evil, He will use for good." I couldn't accept this truth until I started allowing Yah to father the fatherless through me.

As I drove one of my mentees home after an outing, he turned to me in frustration and asked, "How can God have a purpose for my life when my father isn't in it?" Tony had a major father wound, and he had reached a point where he could no longer restrain his emotions.

In love I responded, "Son, do you think I would be here with you right now if my father had stayed with my mother and me? Do you think I would have the unrelenting passion to help uninitiated and fatherless boys?"

He turned to me with teary eyes and said, "No."

I continued, "Tony, it was never God's intention for your father to abandon you; that was your dad's decision. But God loved you so much that He made sure someone like myself merged into your lane to guide you into the life He always desired for you. Yes, it hurts not to have the man you came from take interest in you, but when we push through our emotions, we will discover that our dads were just common vessels— and we came from Yah." He nodded his head in agreement, confirming that my words comforted his heart. We joked and laughed the rest of the ride home.

If you are a divorced father, please realize that your son needs you more in his life than in his house. The conflict you may still have with his mother is not worth the years you'll waste if you're not being a positive influence in your son's life. And if you are fatherless yourself, please be encouraged by my testimony. That part of your life might have been meant for evil against you, but Yah will use it for good. This is truly a spiritual war, and we must trust Yah's perfect and permissive will for our lives, allowing Him to father us through trauma so that we do not repeat it with our sons. We must give our sons what we longed for instead of what we lacked.

Many of us today in the African American community do not realize that our fathers were just two or three generations removed from slavery. Their "love language" was to protect and provide, but they did not have the emotional capacity to affirm us. Due to the barbaric beatings, raping of our women, and the parceling of our children to the highest bidder like puppies, our forefathers had to detach their emotional ties in order to survive mentally and physically. And for my brothers from another mother, your fathers had men like John Wayne, Humphrey Bogart, and Clint Eastwood as their role models. They, too, were never taught to express their emotions without fearing condemnation. Frederick Douglass is often attributed as having said, "It's easier to build strong

> **We must give our sons what we longed for instead of what we lacked.**

children than repair broken men." While this is certainly true, it does not mean that we should simply leave men broken.

———————— ≈ ————————

As we wage and win our wars within, we cannot forget the prisoners of this war! *Sankofa* (pronounced *SAHN*-koh-fah), a word in the Twi language of Ghana, means "it is not taboo to fetch what is at risk of being left behind."[3] This action of redemption is symbolized by a bird with its head turned backward, carrying a precious egg in its mouth while its feet face forward. As I shared in my memoir, *Cry Like a Man*, I was thirty-seven years old by the time I heard my father say, "I love you, son" for the first time. This did not happen until I affirmed him and made sure he received my affirmation. I had to reach back and free my father so he could express the words I needed to hear that would heal my heart.

If we are willing to open our hearts and minds to the strong possibility that our fathers did not receive affirmation from theirs, we can break the intergenerational trauma cycle for ourselves—and our sons won't have to struggle the way we did.

But this rescue mission will require us to be courageously transparent and vulnerable because reaching back to free our fathers from emotional incarceration will cause us to revisit the emotional jail cells from which we escaped. Revisiting these memories with our fathers can be painful, but they are part of the healing process. So, let's give our fathers the grace they need to express themselves without fear of condemnation.

We desire earthly affirmation, but we who are spiritual should never allow that desire to deter us from receiving it from the only One who knows our deepest thoughts and can answer all of our questions. Yah promised to be a Father to those without dads. However, I didn't understand how He could fulfill that promise until I allowed Him to father me using the affirmation from other men that finally healed my heart. When we allow ourselves to accept affirmation from the men in our lives, we will break the cycle of emotional emptiness before it continues into future generations.

Receive and Believe

As husbands, this same lack of affirmation makes us vulnerable to our evil desires, luring our hearts away from our wives. When those desires go unchecked, they give birth to sin, and when fully grown, that sin leads to death (James 1:14–16). Sometimes that "death" is divorce. When we do not have adequate affirmation throughout our lives, we are prone to desire it from women who are not our wives. That is also death. But when we allow ourselves to not only receive affirmation from our families and from the Most High but also believe it, we will be able to walk away from temptation when it comes our way.

Years ago, when I was remodeling our first house, I needed to go to Home Depot and purchase a gallon of paint. After picking up my paint order, I grabbed the rest of my materials and headed toward the checkout.

As I walked through the aisles, I noticed a woman staring at me. A few steps later, I heard her say, "You can't paint!"

I kept walking, and she followed me, obviously trying to flirt with me.

"You can't paint. You can't paint!" she yelled as I walked toward the register. At the checkout counter, the woman caught up to me. "You didn't hear me talking to you?" she asked with a flirtatious smile. I know that kind of smile when I see it. I moved away with a closing comment.

"I did hear someone yelling, 'You can't paint,' but since I *can* paint, I did not respond."

She laughed and walked away.

King Solomon once advised his sons to keep their paths far from immoral women (Prov. 5:8). I had no desire to go down that road because Nicole affirms me with her words and actions. My emotional needs in that area are met at home, so there's absolutely nothing a woman can say to me that hasn't already been confirmed by my wife.

In addition to guarding your heart from inappropriate affirmation from women who are not your wife, I encourage you to be careful not to seek affirmation that only feeds your ego. We must learn to live from who we are instead of what we do—only gravitating toward the areas in life we believe we can win in. For example, when people publicly praise us for our work, community service, or ministry, areas where we're doing well, it can make us proud of ourselves. But after the acclamation has been given, many of us go home and feel invisible because our wives and children aren't as excited about what we've done for others. Instead of continuing to try and improve as husbands and fathers, we subconsciously feel that we have to prove our families wrong. So, we relentlessly pour ourselves into any work that garners admiration from our public performance.

I've learned that the biggest issue isn't our failures but

that we don't invest enough time to become better in the places that should matter the most. If we desire affirmation at home, we must be intentional about serving and affirming our families more than we serve those in our workplaces or communities. When I started "watering my own grass" and spending quality time with my wife and children, they eagerly began publicly expressing their love and adoration for me. I don't know about you, but I'd rather be a private success and a public failure than gain all the accolades this world could offer. I'd rather be affirmed for who I am as a husband and father than what I do for a living.

> **If we desire affirmation at home, we must be intentional about serving and affirming our families more than we serve those in our workplaces or communities.**

Lastly, do not allow your past unmet desires to sabotage your present blessings. One exercise that helped me break this stronghold is called "Crowning the King," which is done with a group of men. During this exercise, one person sits in a chair while other men pronounce words of affirmation and praise over him. The man in the chair cannot deflect the affirmation or say a word. He must sit there and receive it. I strongly encourage you to try this exercise with the person you identified in chapter 4 or, better yet, your wife, your sister, or other significant women in your life.

You've fought exceptionally well, warrior, and have defeated almost all the inner enemies in this book, but do not get complacent; you are just a page away from your next battle. Before you shout a battle cry, take a moment to reflect on the emotions you felt during this chapter so you can release the toxic ones and reset. Then be sure to yell, "Milchamah!" as you prepare to wage more war within.

Do not worry. The Enemy does not see you coming, so take the time needed to get mentally and emotionally prepared. This next battle will require you to find and capture something that many men say they desire but rarely do.

TEN

REST NOW OR REST IN PEACE

It is vain for you to rise up early, to retire
late, to eat the bread of painful labors; for He
[Yah] gives to His beloved even in his sleep.
—*Psalm 127:2*

I woke up one Friday morning a few years ago feeling "off." I'd
had two great Brazilian jiu-jitsu classes that week, but something didn't feel right. I was no longer shaken by the negative
effects of watching my beloved mother mentally deteriorate
from dementia, but the emotional journey with her had taken
a toll on me physically. I knew something was wrong internally.
My energy was zapped, so I took the advice of a friend and
made an appointment with a holistic doctor.

When I walked into the clinic, I sensed it was a divine
appointment. I could feel Yah's grace covering me as gospel
music filled the waiting room. I soon learned that the holistic
doctor, Obadiyah, was also a pastor. Being leery of naturopathic

methods, I purposefully did not tell him what was bothering me. I figured, if he was good, he would know what was wrong.

He took my blood, urine, and saliva, then proceeded to tell me everything that was going on with my body. He knew which side of my back had been hurting for years. He pointed out my knee injury. I thought he had tapped my phone! You name it, he knew it all just from reading my test results. He then pulled up a picture on a computer monitor and said, "These are your blood cells. This is not good." My blood was agglutinating (clumping together), and my energy reserves were life-threateningly low. I was at the doorstep of a heart attack. He said if I hadn't come in when I did, I probably would have died right after my mom passed in the coming months. The energy spent from caretaking and grieving would have overwhelmed my already stressed heart.

He put me on a strict vegan diet for four months and told me to drink only distilled water. If that wasn't bad enough, his next instruction really made me cringe. He said I needed what most men seem to be allergic to—rest. He said I must rest and/or sleep a minimum of ten hours a day, and I was not to lift weights during this time period due to my tapped energy reserves. He even went so far as to say that, when I read my Bible, I should turn the pages as slowly as possible. Suddenly, my active, energetic lifestyle looked like a slow-motion video in my mind. Of course, Obadiyah was joking about turning pages slowly, but he wanted to place emphasis on the seriousness of my condition.

"You've got to take care of yourself," he said.

"I don't take care of myself. I take care of others," I responded. I had no idea what taking care of myself meant, but I knew I had to find out before it was too late.

———≈———

In today's grinding culture and people-pleasing society, we see rest as a sign of weakness rather than a restoration of strength. We go and go and go until we literally can't go anymore. Then when our health fails us, we realize our unrelenting quest for "success" derailed us. I now see why men jokingly refer to the toilet as a "porcelain throne," because that's seemingly the only time we can sit longer than five minutes in peace.

Yah's Word says that if a man doesn't work, a man doesn't eat (2 Thess. 3:10). This is a true adage; however, if we never cease work in order to rest, work will rest us in peace. We are worth more than our work! This may sound obvious, but the world we live in constantly and subconsciously tells us that our work determines our value. As a result, countless good men have driven themselves to early graves. And this culture even has our wives and families temporarily deceived until they're planning our funerals. Trust me, if you don't take a break, you will eventually break.

In one of my presentation slides for our Emotional Stability Training on rest, I show images of elderly couples in restaurants, the mall, or around the neighborhood. Almost always, the wife is peppy, energetically moving around as the husband struggles to keep pace with his cane or walker.

If you don't take a break, you will eventually break.

No wonder research shows that, on average, women live longer than men. In fact, by age eighty, 61 percent of those living are women. And in 2010, 82 percent of centenarians were women.[1]

Yes, as men we were created to provide and protect, and the Most High charged us to work, but He also commands us to rest. After the Most High created the heavens and the earth, the sea, and all that is in them in six days, He rested on the seventh day. And He set the seventh day apart and called it the Sabbath (Ex. 20:11). The Hebrew translation of *Sabbath* is "intermission," to *repose*, that is, *desist* from exertion.[2] Clearly, the Most High is not limited by a physical body, but He set apart this day for our benefit.

Grinding Away

Many of us subconsciously know that the grinding mentality is slowly killing us, but the fear associated with failure keeps us working when we need to rest, fighting when we need to seek peace, and worrying when we need to pray. The word *grind* literally means to wear down by abrasion, to reduce to fine particles by crushing or pulverizing.[3] It can also mean to oppress or torment. It's not a coincidence that people who say they are "grinding" or are "on the grind" look worn out—their work is crushing and tormenting them!

Years ago, if someone yelled, "Grinding!" in a machinery shop, the supervisor would sound an alarm to stop all work until the issue was resolved. In our modern, fast-paced lives, we ignore the grinding warnings and substitute energy drinks and coffee for water and rest. This lifestyle leads to anxiety, insomnia, digestive issues, muscle breakdown, high blood pressure, rapid heart rate, and fatigue, not to mention caffeine dependency because you need more and more just to keep going. Though there's nothing wrong with an occasional cup of coffee, keep in mind that caffeine is a counterfeit energy that creates additional stress in our bodies. As a result, men are exhausted, accomplishing their work but not Yah's perfect will for their lives.

I used to be so caught up in the grind that I was afraid to get caught resting. Until I broke free from emotional incarceration, I would anxiously jump up from a needed nap when I heard Nicole come home. I've surveyed many men of different ethnicities and socioeconomic statuses, and it's alarming how many of us are scared to take naps for fear of appearing lazy. This is such a tragedy because I've also asked dozens of women what they think of men taking naps, and all of them said they want their husbands to rest more. Now, you might be thinking, *Yeah, they say that, but these bills are due!* Trust me, I feel you. However, if taking a daily fifteen- to twenty-minute nap stops you from providing for your family, you have a bigger problem.

One afternoon in the CATTA as I was teaching our newly enrolled recruits, I glanced at the stage where the fathers sit and watch. I noticed that all of them looked exhausted. I had planned to teach the boys some basic defenses against an attack, but Yah told me to put my plans on hold and follow His lead. I asked all the fathers to take off their shoes and join their sons on the mats. After briefly discussing the basics of Shalach, I told them all to lie back, close their eyes, relax, and breathe. Within minutes, I could hear one of the fathers snoring. I then quietly tapped each of their sons on the shoulder and had them rise to a seated position. They were all very relaxed.

I looked each of them in the eyes and said, "I can teach you how to fight, but if I do not teach you how to rest, you will not have the energy to fight right." I asked them how it felt to rest after a long day at school. They responded with descriptions such as, "Refreshing," "Good, sir," and "I feel stronger." I then asked them to look at their fathers, who were all in a deep sleep across the mats by this time.

"When was the last time you saw your father rest during the day?" I asked.

Sadly, they all responded, "Never."

As fathers, it's imperative that we teach our sons to have a good work ethic, the principle that hard work is intrinsically virtuous or worthy of reward. However, it's counterproductive if we do not also show them the rest ethic: the principle that rest is crucial for them to work productively. Studies reveal that a lack of adequate rest not only affects your physical health but has a big impact on your mental health as well. Not getting the seven or eight hours of quality sleep you need can heavily influence your outlook on life, energy level, motivation, and emotions.[4]

When I asked the fathers to rise to a seated position, I was amazed at what fifteen minutes had done for them! They all looked refreshed and relieved of the stress that was evident on their faces prior to the exercise.

Before my health scare, I was one of those men who would say, "I would rest, but I have too much to do." That is, until my doctor responded, "Well, I'll see you at your funeral." As a father and husband, I must prioritize self-care if I want to be there for my family. I cannot work the way I did fifteen years ago and expect to have the energy needed to make a positive impact in my home and community.

Warrior, you may believe you do well under pressure, but do not forget you're still *under* pressure. Refuse to allow your work—yes, even your selfless service to others—to cause you to lose your mind, health, marriage, and family. The words "take care of yourself" are not just words to be said when leaving, but wisdom you'd better heed if you want to keep living. Always remember, no one will ever stop you from helping them do more work—so it's up to you to stop grinding and start resting.

Take Off Your Cape

Yah wants us to have an abundant life, but we can't have one if we live our lives trying to make everyone else happy. We have to take the superman cape off because as long as we walk around like a superhero, people will keep asking us to do superhero things. I finally took my cape off, and I have to remind myself daily that I am not superman—I am human.

> The words "take care of yourself" are not just words to be said when leaving, but wisdom you'd better heed if you want to keep living.

Take home improvement, for example. I am skilled with my hands in regard to construction, and as a result, we have a beautiful home, except for that last room in the house that needed a complete remodel—the mudroom. Due to the demands and compassion fatigue associated with my work in the CATTA, filming a documentary, writing books, and speaking at all sorts of events, we budgeted to pay someone to install a porcelain floor and cabinets. But when I tore out the top layer of the existing floor, I discovered that the subfloor needed to be replaced. That repair took us over budget, and I had to install the floor and cabinets myself.

In short, it was like dominoes. The mudroom project turned into the master bedroom project. The master bedroom project turned into the master bathroom project. And the master bathroom project turned into the living room project! Although I knew Nicole desired to renovate all of those rooms, she didn't ask me because she knew how much was on my plate. But after I finished the mudroom, I was driven to fulfill my wife's desires.

I jumped in with both feet to install a new subfloor, porcelain tile, cabinets, countertop, new doors—and it felt good to hear, "That looks great, baby!" But afterward when I was alone, I became overwhelmed with anger because I'd worked a couple of months, ten to twelve hours a day, without a day off. With little to no rest during that time, I ended up physically exhausted and emotionally depleted.

This kind of behavior and subsequent attitude is unfair not only to Nicole and our children but to myself. What I should have said to Nicole was, "Hey, I'm going to remodel the mudroom, and when I feel I have completely rested and recovered, we can start on the master bedroom project." Instead of working to prove my worth, I could have spared myself and my family the pain of resentment, and I could have enjoyed each project without depleting my energy.

It's hard to take the cape off when it becomes your identity. Again, no one will ever stop you from helping them. It's up to you to renounce the superhero lifestyle. Never fret that you will lose your position when you have to temporarily step off the ladder of success to rest from a long work week or heal from emotional pain and/or trauma. Taking time to reflect will not hinder your progress. It will only empower you for a refreshed reentry. But you must take the time.

Keep in mind that Yah cannot fill your cup if you keep moving it!

———— ≈ ————

Believe it or not, when you remove the cape and start taking care of yourself, it's normal to be misunderstood by others, especially when you make the decisions Yah is leading you to make. From Abraham to Yahushua, we see this play out time and time again in the lives of those who subserviently follow the Most High. This is why it's imperative that we know His voice when it's spoken through His people or His Word, so that we will follow Him (John 10:27).

One day during a conversation about introspective reflection and decisions I needed to make, my friend Dr. Tim Broe asked me to ask Yahushua, "What is it You want me to know?" Within seconds after I asked that question, Yahushua said, "I want you to know it's okay. I am with you. Take the needed time to rest and reflect. Have the faith needed to separate the wheat of My will for your life from the chaff of other people's needs for your life. Sort the valuable from the worthless, and then move forward" (Matt. 3:12).

Then the Holy Spirit brought to my remembrance the temporary retirement of Michael Jordan after his father was murdered, which affirmed all of the decisions I had to make regarding self-care and His purpose.

In 1993, Michael Jordan had won three straight NBA titles, three straight NBA Finals MVP awards, and seven straight scoring titles. Just a month after MJ won his third NBA title, his father was shot to death while sleeping in his car. Due to his passion for winning, MJ tried to push the emotions of losing his beloved father to the side in order to win a fourth NBA title. But he couldn't. All appeared to be well with MJ on the outside, but inside he was still deeply grieving the tragic death of his father, James Jordan.

MJ stunned the world when he announced his retirement in 1993, citing a loss of desire to play basketball. His teammates, his fans, and the media wanted MJ to work through his emotional pain and play, but he decided it was best to step away from the NBA. MJ's retirement became more baffling when he signed a minor league baseball contract with the Chicago White Sox. When asked about his seemingly radical decision, Jordan said, "[Baseball] gave me an opportunity to revisit all those moments that I had with my father. . . . It was a therapeutic experience for me."[5]

MJ was willing to risk his future success for what he needed most: introspective time to reflect on memories of his father. When Jordan returned to the NBA in 1995, he was a dramatically changed leader who won three more NBA titles. This mental shift led the 1996 Chicago Bulls to an NBA record for most wins in the regular season (72–10). Jordan did not worry about temporarily stepping off that ladder of success. He needed to heal and rest. Similarly, we should never apologize for taking a day off and resting when we need rest.

Do Not Put the Cape Back On

My beloved mother, Etta Marie Crum, made her transition from hospice to heaven in April 2016. I knew I had given her my all as we walked the last six years of her life hand in hand through the valley of dementia. I truly had no regrets. If you couple that resolution with the peace of Yah that passes all understanding, I was doing exceptionally well. Within two weeks I was back to the busyness of the Yunion and the CATTA.

However, after longing for my mother's presence on Memorial Day, I realized something was wrong. I hadn't grieved! It had only been three weeks since my mom's death, and I had already "people pleasingly" placed one foot back on the hamster wheel of community needs. I hadn't allowed the Most High to establish His process for healing my broken heart.

I praise Yah for this revelation, because it potentially saved my life. He paused His peace because I was allowing the pressure of being needed to hinder me from experiencing His healing presence. I immediately started making the personal and professional decisions necessary to keep my life rooted in His will and not in others' wants. These decisions cost me future opportunities to advance professionally and financially, but I was not emotionally shaken after making them. I've learned through experience and the teachings of Yahushua, that making decisions based on money is unwise. My job is to seek first His kingdom (Matt. 6:33). I felt settled in spirit after making what many would call risky decisions, but my actions were met with sincere skepticism. As Paul Coughlin wrote, "People love the status quo, and when you break from it, like a prisoner over a fence, all kinds of sirens and lights will be thrown on to get you back in the yard."[6]

Although I am martially trained to push through any emotion to accomplish any task at hand for others, I am not a superhero. I chose to heed the Holy Spirit and make the best decisions for myself. I had to walk away from $60,000 in grant funding opportunities for my work in the CATTA. This was a major step for me. We definitely could have used the financial resources; however, the additional responsibilities that came with it would have quickly taken a toll on my health.

So many good men burn themselves out by putting the superhero cape back on and hustling for worth in a world that considers you worthless when you can't do something. Who wants to live a life in which you always have to perform for love or significance? We need to stop seeking unconditional love from humans. Ultimately, that's a dead end—and definitely no fun. Throw your cape in the trash and discover the full meaning of rest.

Finding Fun

I often ask men who attend my workshops to recall the last time they had fun. The majority of men cannot recall a single fun event. I usually get a deer-in-the-headlights response, as if they don't even know what fun is. After a couple of minutes, a few men will speak up and say things such as "When I go to the park with my kids" or "When I go out to eat with my family." Then I say, "No . . . when have you had fun either alone or with your male friends?" They usually can't answer that question.

If you don't allow yourself time for healthy recreational fun, you're missing out on a crucial part of living. Yahushua once said, "Come to me, all of you who are weary and carry heavy burdens, and I will give you rest" (Matt. 11:28 NLT). The word *rest* in this verse translates not only to intermission or cessation from labor but also to recreation. In other words, Yahushua was also saying, "Come to me, and I will give you fun." We need to remember we are human *beings*, not human *doings*.

Here's an example from my own life. One sunny afternoon, my friend Aaron asked me to go with him to look at bikes for cycling. Although I wanted to experience fun again and deeply desired male companionship, I always seemed to sabotage every opportunity to do either. But this time I followed my feeling. When we arrived at the bike shop, I was amazed at how bikes have evolved from the eighty-pound Toys"R"Us specials. Aaron grabbed a bike he was interested in buying and told me to pick one so we could take a test ride.

Due to the design of these bikes, pedaling felt effortless as we reached speeds near twenty-five miles per hour. As the wind blew on my face, I felt something different. *What is this feeling?* I wondered. Then I heard Yah say, "It's called fun." I chose to purchase that bike, and it's one of the most responsible things I've ever done in my life. Now when I feel overwhelmed, I take an early morning or night ride on my bike as I shalach the cares of the day.

Since then, I have realized the benefit of fun and recreation in my life, and I also see it in the lives of my friends. Due to my desire for camaraderie, I purchased a bike rack for my truck that can hold four bikes in case any of my friends want to join me for a ride. One day, a close friend of mine called and said that he was so upset at his wife he needed to leave the house. I said, "Okay, grab your bike. I am about to come pick you up." As we cycled around the park, he began to relax almost instantly. We talked, we did Shalach, and I helped him reflect, release, and reset. By the time I took him home, his anger toward his wife had subsided.

Can you imagine how much enjoyment we as men could have in our lives if we did that every week? Another close friend of mine, Duante, rents a boat and gets up early to go fishing and relax. Then he gets home by 10:00 a.m. and still has time to spend with his kids. Because he does that for himself, he is able to respond to his family in love. He says he laughs more since he adopted that practice, and he's able to do other things more from his heart than from being tense and thinking everything is based on being responsible. As men, when we find fun again and implement it in our lives often, we become better fathers, better husbands, and more effective community servants.

In the sport of football, when a team is leading with limited time remaining, they will execute plays designed to run the game clock out or leave the other team with little to no time to score if they get the ball back. As the saying goes, the best way to stop a powerful offense is to keep them off the field.

In life, one of the best ways to delay the man of the Most High from accomplishing Yah's will is to keep him grinding. It's true that, "When someone has been given much, much will be required in return; and when someone has been entrusted with much, even more will be required" (Luke 12:48 NLT). But it's hard for Yah to use us if we're always tired.

Just Say No

As cliché as it sounds to "just say no," these are wise words worth repeating. Nicole recently asked me, "Why do you always say no when someone asks you for something?"

I replied, "If I say no, I can always come back and say yes after I've thought about it. But if I say yes first, I have to fulfill that promise." The Scriptures say, "Let your 'Yes' be 'Yes,' and your 'No,' 'No'" (Matt. 5:37 NKJV). A man of the Most High should never feel pressured into spontaneously reacting to someone's request but instead should always allow himself the liberty to process the potential results of a decision before he makes one (Luke 14:28).

When you wake up and change, people may complain and ask you to keep grinding. Simply say no. In the movie *The Matrix*, I love the ending fight scene when the agents fire bullets at Neo. Because Neo now knows who he is, he resolves to stand still and deflect their ammunition. I imagine each of those bullets representing words such as *people pleasing, anxiety, fear of failure,* and *stress.* As the bullets make their way toward Neo in slow motion, Neo holds his hand out and says, "No."

> **It's hard for Yah to use us if we're always tired.**

The look of determination on his face is priceless as the bullets stop, suspended in midair. He reaches out to grasp one of the bullets with his fingers, looks at it curiously for a moment, then drops it to the floor. The rest of the bullets fall to the floor like rocks as the agents stare at Neo in awe.

The worst thing you can do is everything. As I said before, nobody will ever stop you from helping them—but you can. Take care of yourself! Learn to say no to people pleasing, self-doubt, fear of failure, and other toxic emotions and thoughts that keep you going when you need to rest.

In the last part of this scene, one of the agents runs toward Neo to attack him. Neo calmly thwarts his attack, deflecting all of his punches. Then with a side kick, Neo sends the agent flying backward and crashing to the cement floor. End game. In your real life, these agents (emotions and thoughts) will rise again, but with self-care practice, you can rule them!

What does self-care look like? Here are my five simple rest reminders:

- **Sleep.** Get a minimum of seven hours of sleep every night and take a fifteen-minute power nap every day.
- **Shalach.** Spend at least five minutes both in the morning and at night meditating and casting your cares on Yah.
- **Speak.** Talk to a counselor a minimum of four times a year. Speak with a friend, a mentor, or a coach even more often.
- **Say no.** Practice saying no before you say yes. Try this first in the mirror or with a friend. People may not like this new you at first, but trust me, they will eventually respect your boundaries for self-care.
- **Seek fun.** Make time for simple recreation weekly, if not daily. Fishing, playing sports, cycling, and ATVing are often favorites among men. Be sure to participate in activities that make you laugh as well.

Now, arise warrior; you've had enough rest and recreation to physically and mentally recuperate for this last battle. The life you've longed to live is just before you, but the Enemy has surrounded it with the fortified walls of your past emotional pain and trauma. These barriers cannot be demolished until you face them and learn to forgive. So, shout a battle cry and yell, "Milchamah!" because the next battle is the last for a reason—you will need to apply all that you've learned in order to win the war within.

ELEVEN

LET GO AND LIVE

Time doesn't heal all pain, you
need to learn how to let go.
—ROY T. BENNETT, *THE LIGHT IN THE HEART*

One sunny afternoon in 1981, I walked to our neighborhood supermarket to buy some Chips Ahoy! cookies—my favorite snack. After I made my purchase, I eagerly exited the store to begin my route back home. It was never a surprise to see a stray dog in my neighborhood, but for some reason, the one sitting outside the store struck fear in my heart. Instinctively, I started running—fast! And the dog, a medium-sized German shepherd, started chasing me.

I was eleven, and I had the stamina to run around the perimeter of the market one time, but I was gassed shortly thereafter. I finally figured I would have to fight this dog if

I was going to make it home. I stopped, turned around, and stood in a fighting stance. To my surprise, the dog stopped too. After a twenty-second stare down, I figured it was safe to turn and start my journey back home. But as soon as I started walking, the dog followed. I started running again, and the dog took chase! He trailed me halfway around the market again until I couldn't run anymore. While gasping for air, I turned around and held my fists up, ready to fight again. The dog slowed to a standstill and stared at me just like before.

By this time, I realized the dog was only chasing me because I was running, and the energy I exerted trying to get away could have gotten me home twice. Once I resolved in my spirit that this dog was no threat, I confidently turned and started my journey home. As expected, the German shepherd followed me for about fifteen feet but stopped just before I left the parking lot of the supermarket.

Decades later, I look back on that day and wonder how often we allow our traumatic pasts to chase us in our present lives. When we mentally run from past wounds and traumatic experiences instead of facing them, we hinder ourselves from experiencing the life we desire. Every time we look back, we re-traumatize ourselves. But there comes a time in life when we have to stop running and let go of what lies behind us in order to live.

> **There comes a time in life when we have to stop running and let go of what lies behind us in order to live.**

Our past is just that—the past—and it's always confined to that moment in time as long as we do not allow our past trauma to time travel.

Just as the German shepherd in the grocery store parking lot was not a real threat, neither are our past experiences—unless we allow them to be. When I stopped running from the emotional pain I experienced with my father, coldhearted women, and disloyal friends, I was able to heal and appreciate my present life.

I was also able to prevent the intergenerational transmission of trauma to my children. As difficult as it was to stop running from the hurt and trauma of my past, I really didn't start living until I let those traumas go by forgiving those who caused them.

The Fortitude to Forgive

For most of life, I thought forgiveness made men look milksop because it always appeared as a form of surrendering to those who did you wrong; you were excusing their actions. If anyone had a right to resent other people, I certainly did. In 1935, six racist and wicked-hearted white men kidnapped, beat, and lynched my grandfather. The hurt I felt compelled me to justify hatred for all white people, but that kind of enmity and blind rage had the potential to turn me into someone just like the men who murdered my granddad. My life experiences with people of other ethnicities, though, some being dear friends and loved ones, have shown me that no cultural group is innately evil.

I'm not saying forgiveness is easy, but holding on to offenses will keep you trapped in emotional incarceration. I've seen firsthand the heart-wrenching side effects of holding on to trauma. Four out of six of my mother's siblings suffered with dementia, and one struggled with alcoholism. I believe if my grandfather could speak to me today, he would say, "Grandson, it's honorable for you to look back and reflect on my life. However, if you do not let go of the emotional pain associated with my death, you, like your mother and the rest of my children, will never be able to live your own life freely."

Instead of allowing my anger to fuel hatred for a race of people, I chose to use my feelings to honor my granddad by exposing the evil of racial injustice. If I had allowed my hurt and anger to coerce me to fight fire with fire, I would not be able to put out the fires in the lives of boys and men that I do today.

It's easy to think that withholding forgiveness serves as punishment toward someone who has wronged you, but psychologically, you're only doing more damage to yourself than they originally did. Why? Because choosing not to forgive is like a man drinking poison and expecting your enemy to die.

But forgiveness is a gift from Yah that releases us from the wounds that hold our mental and emotional health hostage. It's a choice we make for our own good and a key that unlocks the door to a life free of regrets and resentment.

Forgiveness: What It Isn't and What It Is

When choosing to forgive, it's important to understand what forgiveness is not. First, it is not approving of someone's words or deeds. You're not excusing or overlooking their actions. You're not simply "moving on" or pretending nothing happened. Forgiveness is not justifying or letting go of a need for justice. You're not simply "calming down" or sweeping an offense under the rug.

It's also not dependent on the other person or people. You don't have to wait for an apology in order to forgive. Forgiveness is not a restoration of trust, and it's not a one-time event. You may need to repeat your choice to forgive many times before the hurt dissipates altogether.

The old adage "forgive and forget" is a myth. You can't forget what happened in the past, but it's still in your best interest to let it go. In fact, it has been scientifically proven that forgiveness can positively affect your health.

According to Dr. David Puder and the team at the *Psychiatry & Psychotherapy* podcast, forgiveness "changes anxiety to inner peace, reduces symptoms of depression, anger, and paranoia," and may reduce hypertension. It can lead to overall improvement in emotional maturity and increase your capacity for courage and love. It can even alleviate pain from fibromyalgia.[1]

Spiritually, forgiveness is doing unto others as you would *want them to do unto you*—not how they do unto you. How would you feel if someone owed you $50,000 and you forgave them for their debt but later you heard this same person was harassing someone who owed him $20? This is how Yahushua looks at us when, after we've been forgiven, we do not forgive people who have done us wrong (Matt. 18:21–35).

Letting go of offenses keeps us in good standing with the Most High. Yahushua said that if we refuse to forgive others, our Father in heaven will not forgive our sins (Matt. 6:15). The apostle Paul reminded us to "make allowance for each other's faults, and forgive anyone who offends you. Remember, the Lord forgave you, so you must forgive others" (Col. 3:13 NLT).

Let Go of the Blow

One day in the CATTA, I noticed a recruit got frustrated every time I was able to hit him while we were sparring. His frustration would cause him to implode emotionally and drop his guard, making it easy for me to hit him again.

This is what happens when you do not let go of the blow. You have to detach your mind from what happened so you can respond to what's happening. As long as my recruit kept dwelling on the fact that I could hit him in the face, he was unable to recognize and defend against the next punch coming toward his abdomen. Whether it was one minute ago or twenty years ago, if you do not let go, you will keep getting hit.

This plays out the same way in life. If you cannot let go of the memory of a bad relationship with the wrong woman, you'll overlook the right one Yah has placed in front of you.

The key to letting go of any blow—past or present—is forgiveness. Ultimately, it allows you to live in the present moment, and it will free you from emotional incarceration. Remember, letting go of the blow does not mean you allow people to misuse or abuse you. It doesn't give someone permission to continue hurting you. As in any

> **You have to detach your mind from what happened so you can respond to what's happening.**

martial arts sparring match, it's a response that helps you heal from others' actions so you can think clearly about moving forward or away.

Forgive the Unforgettable

As I touched on in chapter 5, David was the young boy from Israel who defeated Goliath, eventually becoming a faithful servant of King Saul. One day when the troops were returning home after David killed the giant, women of Israel began parading the streets and singing, "Saul has killed his thousands, and David his ten thousands!" (1 Sam. 18:7 NLT). This made King Saul furious. He deeply resented the song, and from that day on, Saul kept a "jealous eye" on David (v. 9 NLT). The next day, the Most High sent a tormenting spirit to overwhelm King Saul. In a rage that overtook him without warning, Saul hurled a spear at David, narrowly missing him twice.

And this is where I turn to the reality that sometimes you must forgive even though you can't forget. You can have successes like David did that will cause spears of jealousy and envy to be hurled at you, even from people who love you. I've had many launched my way, and although I was able to avoid getting pinned to the wall, my loved ones' attempts to harm me actually hurt me more. Just as David returned to Saul, I forgave them with the hopes of reconciling the relationships. Unfortunately, like Saul, many still kept a jealous eye on me.

One day when King Saul was sitting at home with a spear in hand, the tormenting spirit from the Most High possessed him again. As David was playing his harp, Saul hurled his spear at him. David successfully evaded the spear for the third time, leaving it stuck in the wall. This time, instead of returning to Saul, David escaped into the night. Saul plotted to kill David many times thereafter, but he was unsuccessful because the Most High was with David.

David and Saul eventually reconciled, but they never were in each other's presence again. Sometimes after forgiving those who hurt you, it's best to move on instead of allowing your faith to be compromised by their beliefs or actions. We know Saul loved David very much (1 Sam. 16:21), but we also know that "bad company corrupts good morals" (1 Cor. 15:33). Saul was a bad leader, and even if he hadn't grown jealous of David, his unrighteous ways could have negatively influenced David's zeal for the Most High. Staying by Saul's side could have possibly prevented David from becoming king, which may be why the Most High sent the tormenting spirit to fall upon Saul.

If my mother had stayed married to my father, I easily could have adopted his verbally abusive and lothario ways, leading to a life of disrespect for women and broken relationships. Staying in an abusive or dangerous relationship is *never* a good thing. And like shadow missions, which you may want so deeply to hold on to, there are some relationships that have divine expiration dates. Over the years, I've learned that my circle of friends didn't necessarily get smaller as I got older but that Yah was showing me who my real allies were. We all have flaws, but there's actually no such thing as a "bad friend." Someone is either your friend or not a friend at all.

You've probably heard it said that those who forget their past are doomed to repeat it. So, even if you forgive someone, don't feel guilty if you do not forget what they've done. In regard to traumatic experiences or emotional wounds, I say, "Forget the past, but don't forget what happened." In other words, don't allow the pain of your past to prohibit you from experiencing peace in the present, but don't be so naive that you allow people to hurt you repeatedly. And by the way, this includes how you treat yourself!

Forgive Yourself

One thing that will hinder you from finally attaining the life you've longed for is desiring to time travel back to your past in order to undo the consequences of your behavior and decisions. It's good to right a wrong, but planning to do so can become mental torture when it is not humanly possible. I used to ride my bike down the block in my old neighborhood and stop in front of the house where Nicole and I started our family. I would lament over all the times I yelled at Alexis and held grudges against Nicole for days, all for the stupidest reasons. Paternal and marital discord were the norm during those years. Thankfully, not all of the memories were bad. I would also reminisce on the times when I didn't have so much to do, when I could simply cut the grass, eat a sandwich, and lie down.

One day during my neighborhood tour, Yah said, "Jason, do not long for Egypt," referring to when He freed the Israelites from slavery under Pharaoh. They complained and wanted to return to Egypt when they felt afraid in the wilderness. It seemed easier to go back to bondage than do what was necessary to enter the promised land. "'If only the LORD had killed us back in Egypt,' they moaned. 'There we sat around pots filled with meat and ate all the bread we wanted. But now you have brought us into this wilderness to starve us all to death'" (Ex. 16:3 NLT).

Each time I rode down that block, I took mental steps back from the life I had worked so hard to attain. Sometimes our mistakes are our best teachers, not our worst enemies. And the only bad mistake is the one we didn't learn from. Instead of holding on to regrets and failures, we need to repent and ask Yah to forgive us. Then we need to forgive ourselves. Remember, there is no condemnation for those who are in Yahushua (Rom. 8:1)—those of us who have accepted His sacrifice on the cross as payment for our sins.

Warriors, please stop looking back and wishing you could go back. You can't, so let it go. The past only exists in your memory, and it doesn't do any good to curse the road that got you where you are today. Leave the past in the past and move toward the life you're now building instead.

> **Sometimes our mistakes are our best teachers, not our worst enemies.**

The more anger, depression, and distress we carry in our hearts toward the past, the less capable we are of abundantly living in the present. So, go higher, go deeper, and forgive! Take a moment now to practice Shalach—*reflect* on the hurt you've caused and received, *release* the negative thoughts associated with what happened so you can forgive from your heart. Then *reset* and breathe—inhale deeply, exhale strongly. Now that you have the fortitude to push through emotional barriers, it's time to go even higher.

Live in Peace

One of my good friends recently helped his cousin relocate to another apartment. In the process of moving, my friend accidentally dropped and shattered an item that had sentimental value to his cousin. She was so upset at him that their relationship has never been the same. My friend told me how he felt condemned. I asked, "Brother, did you purposely drop that item?"

"Of course not," he replied. "But she keeps telling me what I did wrong and will not listen to me."

"Well, you have to let that go," I advised. "Sometimes it's best to let the know-it-alls know it all."

If you've inadvertently harmed someone, whether you hurt their feelings or accidentally broke something, you should obviously apologize for the impact you had on that person. It's also good to do what you can to repair any damage. However, once you've said and done what's right in the situation, it's up to the other person to choose whether they will forgive you or not. Never let anyone hold you hostage for something you have sincerely apologized for.

How many beautiful sunny days have you let slip away because you were stricken with displaced sadness due to a friend, significant other, or family member's inability to forgive you even after you sought counseling to improve your behavior and become a better man? Any good relationship takes reciprocity to be maintained, but unfortunately, some people will expect you alone to put in the introspective work needed to change.

At the end of the day, we can't make everyone happy. When

you're wrong, do your best to make amends, ask for forgiveness, and try to reconcile the relationship. And remember, forgiveness is for the benefit of the forgiver. If someone refuses to forgive you, it's not really your problem. Repent, forgive yourself, and leave the rest in Yah's hands.

Love Always, Fight If You Must

One of the most effective and desirable techniques for executing a submission in Brazilian jiu-jitsu (BJJ) is called the straight armlock, or arm bar. Interestingly, I've witnessed so many BJJ practitioners stay fixated on applying it that they miss the plethora of other techniques that are available. This happens often in life when we do not let go of a shadow mission, a memory, or hurtful words from a loved one—we stay with what we know and we miss out on capturing an opportunity in the moment.

When I was a new student in BJJ, I would hold on to my opponent's arm, struggling and wasting energy for minutes that could have been used to set up another attack. Even though I clearly did not have enough leverage to control my opponent's arm and make him tap, I stubbornly stayed with this one technique.

Fear of losing or losing control is always a top concern during grappling situations. In life, the ways we hold on and waste precious time are similar. We try to attain something, attempt to get back at someone, aim to prove someone wrong—and we miss all other opportunities to use other approaches and live authentically from our hearts.

As you know, I held on to my dream of producing music in my shadow mission. I pursued it for almost twenty years. But when I finally let go of that one dream—let go of the straight armlock—I saw a triangle choke. When I let go of all my failed relationships, I was finally able to see a beautiful marriage, a loving family, the vision of the Yunion nonprofit come to pass, and create the CATTA. I was able to write *Cry Like a Man* and help men break free from emotional incarceration—and I was able to write this book for you to wage and win the war within. My mind was renewed, and I gained a life of hope and purpose.

But first I had to grapple with my painful past. And truthfully, I still have to grapple with it at times because, contrary to popular belief, time does not heal all

> **Love always; fight if you must.**

wounds. I still have hurt in my heart that needs healing. My mind is renewed when I do the introspective work needed to allow Yah to penetrate my heart and purge what still hurts me.

As you continue to wage your own battle within, I urge you to keep letting go. Keep forgiving yourself and others so you can live fully in the present. Letting go is a lifetime journey. Do not allow offenses and spears of jealousy from others to pin you down in life. As I tell my recruits in the CATTA, "Love always; fight if you must."

Congrats, warrior! You've just completed the training needed to defeat your inner enemies every time they arise. And now,

I want you to look ahead. In order for you to start your next journey, you must first cross these troubled waters in front of you. I've already talked about your past of unmet desires, your past that keeps you from peace, and your past of painful consequences. But now we'll look at this body of water I call the "Sea of Your Past." In these deep waters are your child- and adulthood traumas, unresolved anger, mistakes, ego, fears, insecurities, failures, resentment, abandonment, lust, self-condemnation, anxiety, and hopelessness. I, too, had to cross this sea, but I needed help, and you will too.

Please do not misunderstand what I am saying. You undoubtedly have enough weapons to get across, but you may not have *who* you need to stay there. When you started this journey, I didn't want to come off as something I'm not—religious. But you'll need more than a mere man alongside you because no human can help or hold anyone accountable *all the time*. You will need a supernatural Sensei who will never leave you. One who will comfort you through trials and guide you when you're losing your way or when you don't know what to pray.

In the CATTA, we call Him *Rūach Hä Kōdësh*, which is Hebrew for the Holy Spirit, the regenerating power of the Most High Yah! He will help you *love* when you want to hate. Feel *joy* when you're depressed. Feel *peace* when you're troubled. Be *patient* when you're anxious. Show *kindness* when you want to be merciless. Offer *goodness* when you desire evil. Continue in *faith* when you want to give up. Be *gentle* when rage tries to consume you. And become *self-controlled* when you're about to lose it. If you'll allow Him into your life, your body will become His temple, and you will be empowered to overcome every negative emotion that tries to pull you back to where you came from.

As I've fought my own war within, I've come to realize I cannot win it on knowledge alone, wisdom alone, or discipline alone. I had to surrender my life to Yahushua Ha'Mashiach (Jesus the Messiah, the Anointed One) in order to finally experience victory over my past and have an eternal life after this temporal one (John 10:27–28). As I said in the beginning of this book, you will have to wage and win the war within daily. I couldn't do it without the Good Shepherd safely guiding me through my mental minefields and spiritual battles—saving me from my sins within. And since salvation is too serious for you to just verbally articulate as a statement of faith, I've provided a few national men's groups in the resource section of this book that you can reach out to if you so choose. Any one of them can show you how to truly surrender your life to Yahushua and work out your *own* salvation (Phil. 2:12).

You are now ready to cross the Sea of Your Past. But first, I encourage you to take a moment to practice Shalach: inhale deeply, hold your breath for three seconds, now exhale. *Reflect* on all that you've been through on this journey. *Release* every emotion and thought that could discourage you from applying what you've learned. Then *reset* so you can live from the good in your heart and not your fears.

Now, instead of yelling, "Milchamah!" say, "Shalom," the Hebrew word for peace. You will experience more of it from now on. Walk toward the boat positioned at the bank of the seashore. Take this moment in. Cry if you need to—you've been through a lot. However, do not stay here too long, because your inner enemies are planning an ambush. Don't worry, you've beaten them before and will do so again.

After you've gathered yourself, boldly board the boat like

the fully armored warrior you now are—and take launch! Allow the evening breeze to calm your soul as you slice through the waters of your past. You have fought the good fight, now finish the race—the life you've longed for awaits you just ahead. I am proud of you . . . so proud of you, my friend. You are now ready to wage and win the war within.

A FINAL WORD

Warrior, I've given you all that has helped me wage and win my own daily battles. I emptied my cup in hopes of seeing the Most High overflow yours. Your journey of introspection and healing is up to you now. "Faith without works is useless" (James 2:20), so please do not let this training be in vain. Apply what I've given you and experience the life you have longed for. Live freely from the good in your heart and not your fears. Shalom.

RESOURCES

Cry Like a Man Website: www.crylikeaman.com
This is a comprehensive website for men to learn how to "cry" while being sharpened by other men in a safe space. Here you'll find inspirational and informational blogs and videos, emotional and mental health resources, forums, and support groups in your area.

The Crucible Weekend: www.thecrucibleproject.org
Unlike other Christian men's retreats, The Crucible Project's weekend for men will "challenge you to take a hard look at what is and is not working in your life." You'll wrestle with God in a safe space, discover new truths about yourself, and embrace your God-given masculinity. Man by man, this work is "changing hearts, marriages, families, churches, careers, and cities."

Edge Venture: www.edgeventure.org
This incredible experiential retreat uses biblical principles

and proven communal techniques to help men connect with the Holy Spirit and look at the things that are preventing them from living liberated lives.

K.I.N.G.: www.kingmovement.com
K.I.N.G. is a national nondenominational Christian movement that strengthens men in their personal relationship with Jesus Christ "by providing brotherhood, encouragement, accountability, knowledge, and fellowship," according to the "About" page on their website. The acronym stands for Knowledge, Inspiration, and Nurture through God. K.I.N.G. seeks to "unite true Bible-believing Christian men across racial, denominational, generational and political lines."

National Alliance on Mental Illness:
https://www.nami.org | 800-950-6264
NAMI is the National Alliance on Mental Illness, the nation's largest grassroots mental health organization dedicated to building better lives for the millions of Americans affected by mental illness.

National Suicide Prevention Lifeline:
www.suicidepreventionlifeline.org | 800-273-8255
According to the "We Can All Prevent Suicide" page on the National Suicide Prevention Lifeline website, "Suicide is not inevitable for anyone. By starting the conversation, providing support, and directing help to those who need it, we can prevent suicides and save lives."

ACKNOWLEDGMENTS

The Most High Yah: Although I have so much to be grateful for, especially You teaching me how to wage and win the inner war—I'd rather spend this time praising You than thanking You. You are the sustainer of my soul, the source of my daily joy and peace. It's only in You that I live, move, and have my being. Your love is unrivaled, and Your mercy is unceasing. I stay in awe of who You are and amazed at what You do; no other gods come close to You. I praise You for ordering my steps and my stops. I praise You for gracefully orchestrating my tests and my trials. I praise You for prompting me to pray to be broken. Now I understand who I am here to please. For I know that with one sin, I could be abandoned by everyone and lose everything. But through Your Son, Yahushua, I can repent unto You, and You will eagerly return unto me. HalleluYah!

Nicole: You have been the pillow for my tears and shelter when I had fears. When I felt like I was losing my mind or that my heart could no longer endure the Most High's calling for my life, you prayed and stayed by my side—encouraging me to keep going. You never discouraged my dreams or desires, and whenever Yah gave me a vision to do something, you'd *always* ask, "How can I help you to get it done?" Oh, how I praise the Most High for you—truly I found what is good and obtained favor from Him when I married you! There's no one I would rather be on this journey with than you, and when I die, I pray that Yah will allow us to be together in eternity too. I love you with all of my heart.

Alexis: My beloved, intelligent, talented, spiritually gifted, beautiful Yah-fearing daughter in whom I am well-pleased— you never cease to amaze me! There's absolutely nothing else you could do to make me prouder. Thank you for not only being a source of joy throughout my life but also always having my best interest at heart. I love you so much!

Jason: My beloved son in whom I am well-pleased. I couldn't have prayed for a better son! When you were born, Yah used you as a pacifier to calm my trauma-filled mind and ease the emotional pain of seeing my mother deteriorate mentally from dementia. And today as a young man, you are my best friend, *Chazaq AriYah*—my strong lion of Yah! I love you deeply, my son.

Sinclair: I can say without reservation that without you being the only light of Christ in my young adult life, I would not be the radical man of the Most High I am today. Your decades of prayers, coupled with active love, guided me to light when I was lost in this dark world. Thank you, my beloved brother, for modeling faith instead of just preaching it. I love you.

Olivia: My beloved, intelligent, and beautiful little sister, thank you for always being a source of encouragement. You have no idea how your words of affirmation throughout the years helped me push through my insecurities and fears. I love you and am thankful for your love.

Ronald: My brother from another mother! No one can match the loyalty and love you have shown to me and my family over the nineteen years of our brotherhood. Thank you for always, and I mean always, being there—whether in deed or in prayer! I love you, bro!

Vic: Thank you for making me laugh when my heart was heavy, listening when I needed to vent, and helping when I needed a hand. You have always been more than a friend; you are my brother and I love you!

Duante: You are the closest to a best friend that I have in my life today, and I am so grateful for our camaraderie. Thank you for being a friend that sticks closer than a brother. I love you and your family!

Chris: My spiritual son and an answer to years of prayer. Thank you for always having my back during the times when I needed a mental and physical break from teaching—your faithfulness is unmatched. You will definitely do greater things than I, and I cannot wait to see how Yah uses you!

To all of my family and friends who loved me, prayed for me, cried with me, and supported me throughout the years—I humbly thank you and I love you all!

Dr. Tim and Ellie Broe: Thank you for pouring sacrificially into not only Nicole and me, but our entire family! You both are a godsend, and words will never be able to express our gratitude for what you've done for us. I love you dearly.

Chris Park: I will never forget our first phone call—we connected instantly! It was clear Yah had crossed our paths for His glory, and today it's confirmed. Thank you so much for believing in me as an author—your advice helped me push through and write this book during one of the most challenging times in history. You are the best agent I could have ever prayed for and someone I can confidently call my friend.

Alice Crider: Thank you for being a constant source of encouragement as I allowed Yah to completely use me as His pen. Your calm and confidence helped me press through my concern regarding writing this book with such a short turnaround, especially during a pandemic. Your coaching and editing helped me see that the light at the end of each chapter was actually rays from the sun, and not a train coming. You are truly a gem from Yah, and I am so thankful for our friendship!

Jessica Wong Rogers: Thank you for not only believing in me but always going above and beyond to make sure my voice and vision for this book would stay true to Yah's purpose for it! Your passion, leadership, kind spirit, and professionalism confirm why the Most High chose Nelson Books to publish this book. You are an amazing person, and I hope we can do this again!

My Nelson Family: Thank you, Brigitta Nortker, Jamie Lockard, Rachel Tockstein, Karen Jackson, Sara Broun, Kristina Juodenas, Kristen Sasamoto, and Whitney Bak! Since day one, you all made me feel special, and I am so grateful to be on a team with such an amazing group of women!

NOTES

Introduction

1. *The Lion King*, theatrical ed., directed by Roger Allers and Rob Minkoff (Burbank, CA: Walt Disney Pictures, 1994), 24:08, https://www.amazon.com/gp/video/detail/amzn1.dv.gti.04aea986–29c4-d46f-e8b1-dbb935c22db6.
2. "Suicide Statistics," American Foundation for Suicide Prevention, https://afsp.org/suicide-statistics/.
3. Jonathan Strickland, "Are Men More Violent Than Women?," HowStuffWorks, September 13, 2010, https://science.howstuffworks.com/life/inside-the-mind/emotions/men-more-violent.htm.
4. Steve Neavling, "Michigan Now Ranks Third in Coronavirus Deaths in U.S. as Fatalities Double Every 2 Days," *Detroit Metro Times*, April 1, 2020, https://www.metrotimes.com/news-hits/archives/2020/04/01/coronavirus-deaths-double-in-michigan-in-2-days-reaching-337.

Chapter 1: Escaping Emotional Incarceration

1. Jane E. Brody, "Biological Role of Emotional Tears Emerges Through Recent Studies," *New York Times*, August 31, 1982, https://www.nytimes.com/1982/08/31/science/biological-role-of-emotional-tears-emerges-through-recent-studies.html.
2. "Fear," MP3 audio, 2:16, track 7 on Drake, *So Far Gone*, Cash Money Records, 2009.
3. Cliff Pinckard, "Cleveland Facebook Killing: Where We Stand

Monday Morning," Cleveland.com, April 17, 2017, https://www
.cleveland.com/metro/2017/04/cleveland_facebook_killing_whe
.html.

4. Blue Letter Bible Lexicon, s.v. "milchamah," Strong's H4421, https://
www.blueletterbible.org/lang/lexicon/lexicon.cfm?t=kjv&strongs
=h4421.

Chapter 2: Misconstrued Masculinity

1. Dictionary.com, s.v. "masculine," https://www.dictionary.com
/browse/masculine.

2. Thesaurus.com, s.v. "masculine," https://www.thesaurus.com
/browse/masculine.

3. Nelson Mandela, *Long Walk to Freedom* (New York: Little Brown,
1994).

4. "Health and Well-Being Benefits of Plants," Ellison Chair in
International Floriculture, Texas A&M AgriLife Extension, https://
ellisonchair.tamu.edu health-and-well-being-benefits-of-plants/.

5. Leah Campbell, "Why So Many Men Avoid Going to the Doctor,"
Healthline, September 14, 2019, https://www.healthline.com
/health-news/why-so-many-men-avoid-doctors.

6. "Prostate Cancer: Statistics," Cancer.Net, January 2020, https://
www.cancer.net/cancer-types/prostate-cancer/statistics.

Chapter 3: Putting Peace in Perspective

1. Jimmie Davis Compton Jr., *Chisel Me, Lord!: An Exposition on
Spiritual Formation* (Detroit: Lulu Press, 2015), 328.

2. Blue Letter Bible Lexicon, s.v. "shalach," Strong's H7971, https://www
.blueletterbible.org/lang/lexicon/lexicon.cfm?t=kjv&strongs=h7971.

Chapter 4: Courageous Transparency

1. Anna Menta, "Michelle Obama Lectures Men: 'Y'all Need to Go Talk
to Each Other,'" *Newsweek*, November 1, 2017, https://www
.newsweek.com/michelle-obama-lectures-men-698887.

2. Christopher Pappas, "5 Tips to Use the Plutchik's Wheel of Emotions
in eLearning," eLearning Industry, September 28, 2015, https://
elearningindustrycom/5-elearning-tips-use-plutchiks-wheel-of
-emotions.

3. Lucy E. Cousins, "Are There Downsides to Always Trying to Be
Positive?," *Health Agenda*, HCF, February 2018, https://www.hcf.com

.au/health-agenda/body-mind/mental-health/downsides-to-always
-being-positive.

4. Benjamin P. Chapman et al., "Emotion Suppression and Mortality
Risk Over a 12-Year Follow-Up," *Journal of Psychosomatic Research* 75,
no. 4 (October 2013): https://doi.org/10.1016/j.jpsychores.2013.07.014.

5. Elizabeth Scott, "The Overwhelming Benefits of Power Napping,"
Verywell Mind, January 2, 2020, https://www.verywellmind.com
/power-napping-health-benefits-and-tips-stress-3144702.

Chapter 6: Purging Passivity

1. Paul Coughlin, *No More Christian Nice Guy* (Bloomington, MN:
Bethany House Publishers, 2007), 28.

2. *Avengers: Age of Ultron*, directed by Joss Whedon (Burbank, CA:
Marvel Studios, 2015), 1:43:25.

3. Senior Airman Jarrod R. Chavana, "Communication Wins Wars,"
U.S. Air Forces Central, March 8, 2010, https://www.afcent.af.mil
/News/Features/Display/Article/223904/communication-wins-wars/.

Chapter 7: Combat Communication

1. Dictionary.com, s.v "trigger-happy," https://www.dictionary.com
/browse/trigger-happy.

2. James R. Detert and Ethan Burris, "Don't Let Your Brain's Defense
Mechanisms Thwart Effective Feedback," *Harvard Business Review*,
August 18, 2016, https://hbr.org/2016/08/dont-let-your-brains
-defense-mechanisms-thwart-effective-feedback.

3. "2 Men Dead in Ionia Road Rage Incident," live report by Dani
Carlson (Ionia, MI), video shared by WOOD TV8, September 18, 2013,
on YouTube, https://www.youtube.com/watch?v=IMu5WiPtSZg.

4. Kira S. Birditt et al., "Marital Conflict Behaviors and Implications
for Divorce Over 16 Years," *Journal of Marriage and Family* 72, no. 5
(October 2010): https://doi.org/10.1111/j.1741–3737.2010.00758.x;
Irina Baechle, "Lessons from a Couples Therapist: ConflictAvoidance
Can Destroy Your Marriage," PsychCentral, January 16, 2019, https://
psychcentral.com/blog/lessons-from-a-couples-therapist-conflict
-avoidance-can-destroy-your-marriage/.

5. Christie Hunter, "The Negative Effects of Unforgiveness on Mental
Health," Theravive, April 28, 2014, https://www.theravive.com/today
/post/the-negative-effects-of-unforgiveness-on-mental-health
-0001467.aspx.

6. *Avengers: Infinity War,* directed by Joe and Anthony Russo (Burbank, CA: Marvel Studios, 2018), 1:23:29.

Chapter 8: Sexual Self-Control

1. Blue Letter Bible Lexicon, s.v. "`azar," Strong's H5826, https://www .blueletterbible.org/lang/lexicon/lexicon.cfm?t=kjv&strongs=h5826.
2. Cambridge English Dictionary, s.v. "succor," https://dictionary .cambridge.org/us/dictionary/english/succor.
3. Rebecca Ruiz, "How Childhood Trauma Could Be Mistaken for ADHD," *The Atlantic,* July 7, 2014, https://www.theatlantic.com /health/archive/2014/07/how-childhood-trauma-could-be-mistaken -for-adhd/373328/.
4. Christian Nestell Bovee, *Intuitions and Summaries of Thought,* vol. 1 (Cambridge, MA, 1862), 178.
5. https://www.wcsap.org/help/about-sexual-assault/how-often-does-it -happen; https://mainweb-v.musc.edu/vawprevention/research/ mentalimpact.shtml; https://www.womenshealth.gov/relationships -and-safety/sexual-assault-and-rape/college-sexual-assault.

Chapter 9: Accepting Affirmation

1. Jason Wilson, "Cry Like a Man w/ Jason Wilson," interview by Van Lathan, January 22, 2019, in *The Red Pill,* podcast, MP3 audio, 1:26:26, https://www.pandora.com/podcast/description/van-lathans -the-red-pill/047-cry-like-a-man-w-jason-wilson/PE:2985540.
2. https://www.blueletterbible.org/lang/lexicon/lexicon.cfm?Strongs =H8597&t=niv.
3. "The Power of Sankofa: Know History," Carter G. Woodson Center, Berea College, https://www.berea.edu/cgwc/the-power-of-sankofa/.

Chapter 10: Rest Now or Rest in Peace

1. Emily Brandon, "What People Who Live to 100 Have in Common," *U.S. News,* January 7, 2013, https://money.usnews.com/money /retirement/articles/2013/01/07/what-people-who-live-to-100-have -in-common.
2. Blue Letter Bible Lexicon, s.v. "shabbath," Strong's H767, https://www .blueletterbible.org/lang/lexicon/lexicon.cfm?t=nasb&strongs=h7676.
3. Dictionary.com, s.v. "grind," https://www.dictionary.com/browse /grind.
4. The National Sleep Foundation, "Excessive Sleepiness," Sleep

Disorders, SleepFoundation.org, https://www.sleepfoundation.org
/excessive-sleepiness.

5. *Michael Jordan: Above and Beyond*, directed by Michael Winik,
starring Michael Jordan (Team Marketing, 1996), 16:55, 20:01,
https://www.amazon.com/Michael-Jordan-Above-Beyond/dp
/B00OWQCXJY.

6. Paul Coughlin, *Unleashing Courageous Faith* (Bloomington, MN:
Bethany House Publishers, 2009), 63.

Chapter 11: Let Go and Live

1. David Puder, "Episode 042: The Science Behind Forgiveness and
How It Affects Our Mental Health," *Psychiatry & Psychotherapy*,
April 10, 2019, https://www.psychiatrypodcast.com/psychiatry
-psychotherapy-podcast/2019/4/10/what-is-forgiveness.

ABOUT THE AUTHOR

Jason Wilson is the founder and CEO of the Yunion (pronounced *union*), a nonprofit youth development organization in Detroit, Michigan. He is also the director of the Cave of Adullam Transformational Training Academy and the author of *Cry Like a Man*. He received the President's Volunteer Service Award from President Obama for his work with youth in Detroit and was the inspiration for an award-winning episode of the hit TV show *This Is Us*. Jason has over twenty-five years of martial arts experience in addition to over fifteen years of training and developing young black males. He is a faithful husband of more than twenty-three years and a proud father of two beautiful children.